BUILD A BETTER YOU
–STARTING NOW!

BUILD A BETTER YOU —STARTING NOW!

3

VINCE BARTOLONE

SHEILA L. MURRAY

FRANK BASILE

GERARDO JOFFE

DAVE GRANT

JERRY V. TEPLITZ

BARBY EIDE

VANCE D. NORUM, Ph.D.

J. BARRY PATCHETT

LUNDA HOYLE GILL

DENNIS B. ADAMS

TOM HAWKES

R. L. MONTGOMERY

ROBERT X. LEEDS

DONALD M. DIBLE, Series Editor

CAROL FOREMAN BROCKFIELD, Senior Editor

SHOWCASE PUBLISHING COMPANY

Fairfield, California

Library of Congress Catalog No. 79-63064
ISBN 0-88205-202-0

Printed in the United States of America.

Showcase Publishing Company
3422 Astoria Circle
Fairfield, California 94533

Distributed to the retail trade by
Elsevier-Dutton, Inc., New York

First Printing

TABLE OF CONTENTS

PREFACE

Hello. We at the Showcase Publishing Company are truly delighted to be able to bring you this third volume in our series *Build A Better You—Starting Now!* I'd like to use this opportunity to tell you just a little bit about this volume, this series, and our publishing company.

First, a word about this volume. Here you have the opportunity to benefit from the motivating, inspiring, and enthusiasm-generating ideas of 14 of North America's most exciting platform personalities—speakers whose messages are heard in person or on cassette by hundreds of thousands of people every year. Now you have the opportunity to read transcripts of their most popular talks and share their most carefully thought-out ideas and discoveries as they commit their observations to the printed page. These messages are now available for the first time in book form. *Build a Better You—Starting Now! Volume 3* is that book—the third in a planned series of 26 volumes.

Next, a word about this series. A full year of motivational, inspirational and self-help "vitamins."—that's the idea behind this 14-chapters-per-volume, 26-volume series. That's a full year's supply of mental nourishment to be consumed at the rate of one chapter per day for 365 days. (Volume 26 will contain 15 chapters, for a total of 365 chapters.)

Drawing from the best of the tens of thousands of established and fast-rising stars in the self-help speaking field, this series is dedicated to bringing to wider and wider audiences throughout the world a vital message: You can build a better you—starting now! With proper guidance, if you are truly dedicated, you can make it happen.

Finally, a word about the Showcase Publishing Company. Showcase was launched by the founders of The Entrepreneur Press, an 8-year-old company dedicated to publishing books for new and small business owners. (One of our titles, *Up Your OWN Organization!—A Handbook on How to Start and Finance a New Business* has sold more than 100,000 copies.) All of the customers of The Entrepreneur Press are interested in self-help information. However, as we came to appreciate that a far larger audience existed for self-help information directed at personal development, the decision was made to start a new company dedicated to serving this larger audience.

As a public speaker myself (I regularly present more than 100 seminars a year), and as a member of several associations of public speakers, I realized that my fellow speakers could provide an enormous amount of material for the new audience we had chosen to serve. It was at this point that we decided to start Showcase. We sincerely hope that you will agree that we did the right thing.

Should you, or someone you know, be interested in contributing material to one of our future volumes, please don't hesitate to write to us. We look forward to hearing from you.

DONALD M. DIBLE
Publisher and Editor-in-Chief
SHOWCASE PUBLISHING COMPANY
3422 Astoria Circle
Fairfield, California 94533

BUILD A BETTER YOU
–STARTING NOW!

VINCE BARTOLONE

Vince Bartolone, the "if it is to be, it is up to me" man, is one of America's leading speakers and writers in the fields of personal development, real estate investment, and the creation of wealth.

His popular book, *Your Million Dollar Success Blueprint,* and his many seminars held nationwide have helped to put thousands of sincere opportunity-seekers on the road to financial independence. This is no small accomplishment for a man who was born poor and never went to school beyond the eighth grade. He has had to apply an "it's up to me" approach to his entire life.

Vince Bartolone became a millionaire three short years after becoming a real estate investor. He used some of the most innovative ideas, concepts, and tactics ever employed in the real estate investment field. Vince is very proud of his meteoric rise in his chosen field. However, he fully understands that he had to get rich in his mind before he could ever be rich in his finances.

Vince believes in the "secret combination to success"—that is, anything can be yours if you make use of the principles of attitude, goals, time-management, imagination, desire, faith, action, and persistence.

You may contact Vince Bartolone by writing to the International Success Institute, 436 Magnolia Avenue #104, El Cajon, CA 92020; or telephone (714) 440-4541.

THE MILLION-DOLLAR PERSONALITY

by VINCE BARTOLONE

Nothing can keep success from the man who really wants it. My life is living proof.

When I was a child my family was so poor that we did not even have indoor plumbing. But we had a lot of pride and love for each other. This sustained me several years ago, when I stumbled from one meaningless job to another, and I never gave up faith in myself or what I knew I could accomplish. Without knowing it, I was en-route to a powerful discovery: the reason I was not a smashing success had little to do with the jobs I was working at. The reason was me! I had to apply my God-given creative imagination and develop the power of positive thinking before I could ever hope to make my goals a reality.

I ultimately chose real estate as the area in which to make my fortune. Real estate was, however, simply the vehicle I used. It was the application of proven success principles that made me a success and a millionaire in less than three years. Anyone who applies these principles can experience success in any career field.

To cultivate the million-dollar mentality you must take control of your life. When asked to reveal my "success secrets," I always name the following principles:

1. Attitude
2. Goals
3. Time-management
4. Imagination
5. Desire
6. Faith
7. Action
8. Persistence

By mastering these principles I became a success. So will you.

Attitude

Attitude is the number-one key to achieving success. To be successful you must cultivate a powerful, positive mental attitude. Positive thinking is the cornerstone for victorious living.

Negativity can survive only in the absence of positive thinking. Your greatest asset in life is you! You must believe in yourself and your unlimited potential.

Everything is for you. There is nothing in this vast and great universe that is against you, believe me! The entire pattern of the universe is positive, expanding, growing, and unlimited. The law of life is the law of success, and it's the law of mind over matter. Your thoughts become your reality! This is why it is so important to prevent negative thoughts, fears, and doubts from entering your consciousness.

If you think that life is against you and holding rewards back from you, the error is in your thinking. Nothing is withheld. All of life's benefits and wealth are available to you. The important question is, how much of this unlimited storehouse of good are you making available to yourself? Your only limit is your own thoughts. Expand your thinking in positive directions and you remove the barriers from your potential growth.

Positive programming. We are all being constantly programmed and reprogrammed. Positive programming is "right thinking," and positive reprogramming reinforces correct mental attitudes. This is *I can* thinking. *I can't* thinking is also ours to choose, but the results are destructive.

Whenever you find yourself in an *I can't* mode, when you find yourself responding with a negative feeling, look at it and reflect on these questions:

1. What purpose did this reaction originally serve?

2. Is it a lasting, meaningful experience, or an unconscious, undesirable one?

3. If you have no sound justification for it, what is your reason to hold on to it?

4. Does this emotional response work for or against your ultimate good? Are you comfortable with it?

This last question is my bottom-line approach to positive mental programming of attitudes. If something is not working in your best interest—discard it! Since negative attitudes never serve our highest interest, we must continue to eliminate them and replace them with the positive factors that assure success.

Remember, your attitude is more important than actual fact. Regardless of how difficult or impossible a situation may appear in realistic assessment, your attitude in the situation is still the most important factor.

There is joy in the active, positive method of "living in the now." The person whose thoughts are loaded with positive mental attitudes is a dynamic, resourceful, creative, and powerful human being—an individual who will experience success.

Overcome your mistakes. One of the tragedies of life is that we have a difficult time accepting ourselves as less than perfect. We dread making mistakes, and when we do, we are often too harsh with ourselves.

The greatness of man is in *the quest to be perfect,* not in perfection itself! Greatness is marred not by mistakes, but only by reluctance to overcome them. You can never be great if you demand that you be faultless.

Thank God for our mistakes, blunders, and errors! They give us the opportunity to learn and grow in the process of rising above them. Human beings are at their very best when they accept a challenge and set out to conquer it.

Goals

Setting and achieving goals and then setting new and bigger ones is the art and science of abundant living.

Setting goals comes naturally to most of us, but achieving goals is a different story. (Do you recall last year's New Year's resolutions? Most folks will not.) The way you approach goal-setting can have a lot to do with whether you will reach your goal. It is important that the goals you select are your own and not the reflection of someone else's aspirations.

It is of equal importance that your goal be positive and ethical—as W. Clement Stone says, "something that will not violate the laws of God or your fellow man." While it is possible to set and reach negative goals, nothing but unhappiness will result. Positive results can be brought about only by positive goal-setting.

Use the law of visualization. A basic, proven law of psychology is that a desire consistently held in mind tends to become objectified in form.

Think about something you want and let it take form in your mind's eye. It can be something as simple as a dashing new car—but not just any car with four wheels, mind you. You have to be specific when you hold an idea in mind and work for it. Decide the make and model and color—whether it's a Volkswagen or a Cadillac, that's up to you. See yourself driving it and get the feel of it. See it as yours, and very soon it will be.

A new home, a car, a vacation, real estate investments—all can be yours if you master the law of visualization. Don't be vague about the things you want. Zero in on your targets. Visualize them in your life and make them reality.

Write down your goals. Many of the greatest goal-setters and goal-achievers tell us to use pen and paper to define our goals. I have found this extremely helpful. There is something powerful in putting goals down on paper. Somehow, by writing them out, we are finalizing our desire and intent and making a total commitment. This is vital to achieving goals.

Time-Management

Another principle that brings success is effective time-management. While I have given time-management an individual classification in my rules of success, it actually is the perfect helpmate to goal-setting. These two are a dynamic duo when used wisely.

There are only 24 hours in each day. No one gets any more or any less. Since most of us sleep 7 or 8 hours, or approximately ⅓ of this time, we all have about the same amount of time for our daily activities. The reason some people find time to reach all their goals while others never find time to finish anything is directly related to time-management. Some people treat their time carelessly, with no thought of conservation. Others measure it out like the precious commodity it is. Time is a key factor in success.

Put yourself on a timetable. People often fail because they try to live their lives in the past or future. True, we should learn from the past and plan for the future, but *the time for action is now.*

The person who falls into the habit of thinking "I'll make my business phone calls tomorrow," or "Five years from now I'm going to have it made," or "I'll reach my sales quota next year," is a person who is not managing time effectively.

Now I'm not saying that it's wrong to set goals for the future. A timetable that includes objectives months or even years away may be constructive. Just keep in mind that a long-range timetable can be productive only if several short-range timetables are in operation at the same time.

Each morning put yourself on a schedule. Remain flexible, since unexpected events can sometimes alter that day's plan. Nevertheless, coordinate your time to your best advantage.

Purchase a daily activity book at a stationery store and keep a small notebook with you at all times. Jot down your daily goals and the time allotted to accomplish each one. This will help you use your time each day to its highest good.

In addition to seven or eight hours of sleep, it is important to set aside time for relaxation and recreation. You will be surprised how much extra time you will find for this once you begin managing your time. Take control of your time, or time will control you. The choice is yours.

Imagination

Everything that we see, feel, taste, or experience was first an idea in the mind. This is why I always tell my students that good ideas put into positive planned action are more valuable than cash or experience. The person with a positive imagination is rich in spirit and also possesses the golden key to financial independence.

Do not confuse creative imagination with aimless day-dreaming. The correct use of creative imagination requires that you take dead aim at those goals you desire. This is the exact opposite of the random thinking that prevents us from centering on our main targets.

Creative excitement. Use your imagination to visualize the accomplishments you desire, and then, for best results, let your creative excitement run wild! Let yourself get really turned on as you imagine all the good things that you accept as rightfully yours. A large dose of creative excitement will give you that extra push to meet your goals on time (or even a little faster than originally expected). Creative excitement is the vivid color that puts your imagination in bright focus.

More than half the fun of making large sums of money, living in a beautiful home, and driving a new car or boat is in the working and preparation for them. It's true! You'll feel great in that home of your dreams, but you will also feel great about yourself as you see yourself coming closer and closer to achieving that home by your own effort. Happy people are forever setting new goals so that their imagination and creative excitement never become dormant. Keep your imagination well fed on a diet of inspiration and new ideas.

Forget past failures—think success. I believe that one of the best human skills is the ability to forget. Memory is a great faculty; the ability to retain information and experiences is very important. But it is also essential to cultivate the ability to *cast out* of the mind thoughts of past failures, unhappy events, and sad experiences. *It's your mind.* You must be very selective about what you keep in it.

Just as there can be positive and negative goals, your imagination can tune in either to images of success or images of failure. Keep your imagination positive and you will benefit.

Desire

I'm very fond of offering the following advice to anyone who has ears and will listen: Anything the mind can vividly imagine, ardently desire, sincerely believe, and enthusiastically act upon must inevitably come to pass. Now every single one of these elements is important— our imagination must be keen, our belief must be intense, and we must be ready to take positive action. However, we still can be defeated if we do not add a large portion of ardent desire.

Most people have a fairly active imagination and can conjure up all sorts of good things to have and enjoy. Some will go so far as to rightfully believe that they should enjoy life's best. But they often lack the sustained, creative, ardent desire that demands results.

Now I'm quite certain you have had a passing desire for many things that have never become reality for you. And you've known many folks who spend their lives desiring all the things that go with health, wealth, and happiness. The big difference between these people and the ones who turn their desires into realities is their *degree of desire*. And a trick of mind is all that separates unproductive passing desire from that positive transforming desire that turns goals into reality.

Your dreams will come true. Anything you really desire, anything you dream of having, is not too great for you to pursue if it will bring happiness and good to your life and cause no harm to others. Never allow anything to cause you to doubt your ability to make your desires reality.

Always make certain that you *truly* want what you desire, for that which you deeply desire and hold in your mind's eye will most certainly be a factor in your life.

One technique to heighten desire is to find good reasons to succeed. Write a list of reasons why you want to do well. The list might include wanting your spouse or parents to be proud of you. Or proving yourself to someone who has been critical of you. Of course the best reason of all to succeed is because you want to and because you'll enjoy it!

Thinking about your reasons for success will activate the adrenalin in your body and the computer in your heart, and they will strengthen your desire.

Faith

Throughout the ages faith has been recognized as a real but unseen power. Religious experience is one form of faith. I believe that faith in God is the greatest expression of faith, but faith is not limited to this one expression. We all have some degree of faith in humankind and in ourselves. This is of utmost importance. The "Million-Dollar Personality" is only a daydream without the power of faith. A person with great faith is a person of great power.

Acquire greater faith. Without faith there can only be fear, uncertainty, and confusion. The person who seeks riches in all forms—spirit, mind, body, and material—cannot tolerate fear and its negative companions.

Throughout history the greatest men and women have been pillars of faith. The explorers who first dared to cross the oceans and discovered new worlds were taking steps of faith. This glorious nation of ours was founded by men and women of ardent faith—people with unrelenting faith in God, in themselves, and in the principles of freedom and national integrity.

All of science is built upon faith. All principles are invisible, and all laws are accepted on faith. True faith is unlimited conviction. It consists of belief in our goals with total acquiescence of the intellect. Nothing is possible without faith. Everything is possible with it.

Action

As necessary as faith, goals, imagination, desire, attitude, and time-management are, you will never be a winner *unless you are willing to take action!*

The certain way to guarantee a better tomorrow is to do everything possible today. Many people decline to act out of possible failure. Yet some of the most successful men I have ever met tasted failure over and over before they finally made it to the top. Many a multi-millionaire has been flat broke at some time.

Just keep in mind that it's one thing to fail and quite another to be defeated. I've failed hundreds of times, but I have never been defeated. Failing does not make failures. Failures are made by giving up. So long as you participate in life and actively pursue your goals, you are not defeated—regardless of how many temporary setbacks you experience. Those who are defeated are those who quit!

"Treat and then move your feet." This is a favorite quotation of those who practice the laws of mind science. It means treat your mind to a picture of what you want, and then get busy working for it. Take affirmative action. It is the "God helps those who help themselves" guide to right action. Believe me, it works!

Ultimate success is achieved by everyday success. If you fail to do one worthwhile thing that you could have done today, you have needlessly failed to advance. We do not foresee all of the results of our actions. Even small, simple acts can reap enormous future benefits. Often what appears to be only a trivial act opens the door for great opportunity. I have learned that little, if anything, happens by accident.

I earned a million dollars in the buying, selling, and trading of real estate. While the actual payoff was brought about by real estate transactions, many little things contributed great success. I relate well with people from all walks of life, from millionaire businessmen to car-wash attendants, from ministers to waitresses. I discovered that my kindness to people and my appreciation of all kinds of folks was often greatly rewarded in advice, tips, and referrals.

Positive action includes making use of every chance

you get to cheer others up, pay a sincere compliment, or give good advice. Little things really do mean a lot, and correct action will always pay dividends.

Be efficient. What you do is equalled in importance by how you do it. Every inefficient action is a setback. *Do not overwork.* This will only lower your proficiency level and possibly harm your health. Long hours of hard work are not the keys to the kingdom of success. Instead, replace hard labor with efficient working habits.

For years I was a pro at working long hours eight days a week. But then I learned better and put what I learned into action: Do each day what can realistically be done in one day efficiently. In doing this, you make each day a successful day.

Living in the now. Trying to live in the past or the future leads to all sorts of problems. Self-expression only works in the present.

The time for your living, loving, and achieving is right now! Don't live a second-hand life. Don't recreate the past or waste time reflecting on fantasies of the future.

Accept yourself as you are now. If you have personality traits that you find undesirable, admit them to yourself and let go of them. Start a fresh, new, abundant life today—right now! *To change your life, you need only to change your mind.* Now's the time to make your life work smoothly.

Choose your friends carefully. I learned a valuable philosophy with the help of a lot of fine people: You tend to become like the people you allow in your environment. Think about this:

- Great people or great minds speak about creative things, such as constructive ideas, success, happiness, and fulfillment.

- Mediocre people or mediocre minds speak of material things, such as "what I did" and "what they did."

- Simple people or simple minds speak of "what I said," "what he said," and "what she said." (This might be termed gossip.)

Choose your friends carefully, because you will become as they are.

Now I'm not condemning anyone. I realize that God loves everyone the same. I'm always willing to give my time to help others. But not everyone wants to be helped. If I see that I'm not making any headway, I simply bless the person and let go. I cannot allow another person's negative thoughts and ways to pull me down—the brain is a computer, and what goes in the brain computer is what comes out.

Scientists tell us that 64,000 bits of information are programmed through the eye-gate of the mind every minute without cease. Wherever I am and whomever I speak with is programmed into my brain computer, and what I learn from them is what comes out. It didn't take me long to figure out that I had better choose a positive, constructive people-environment.

Positive reprogramming. The books *Think and Grow Rich* by Napoleon Hill and *Psycho-Cybernetics* by Dr. Maxwell Maltz are two of the greatest books I have ever read. I thank God that these two great men got my attention and taught me about the brain computer.

Napoleon Hill said, "If you are negative or cannot or do not have faith, then lie to yourself."

This was one of the greatest aids I've ever had. I learned as much as I could about positive affirmation. Then I began "lying" to myself. Every day I told myself: "I am happy. I am wealthy. I am thankful. I can. I have the power—because God gave it to me. Opportunity confronts me daily . . ."

When I began doing this my life exploded! I became very wealthy, healthy, and happy. You don't have to take my word for it—just try it for two or three months and measure the difference. You will be amazed. It will change your life.

A close friend of mine, with whom I've shared my many success secrets over the past years, was at one time poverty-stricken. He was existing on $100 a month by eating beans and spaghetti almost every day. He once fought with a friend over five cents worth of Kool-Aid. Today my friend is worth more than $10 million.

Paul Boileau is his name, and he lives in El Cajon, California. Paul will testify to the fact that these principles of success have rewarded him to the tune of $10 million. Paul understands these concepts now and is so enthusiastic about them that he holds bi-weekly meetings to share his ideas about "the pursuit of the joy and glory of perfection." I would call them discussions on successful living.

At age 39 Paul feels himself getting younger. Believe me, friend, his success was no accident. *He was successful on purpose.* And you can be, too.

Perseverance

Perseverance is the bottom line. It is tied in with action and time-management, but it also remains a separate principle. Without it there can be no true success.

Winners never quit. That wise old saying, "Quitters never win and winners never quit," remains solid-gold truth! You can have many outstanding attributes and still wind up a loser unless you are willing to keep on keeping on. I have seen many people throw in the towel when victory was just a short distance down the road. I have suffered many setbacks in my life. If I allowed myself to accept defeat, I would probably still be picking fruit in Michigan. Instead, I never lost my faith, gave up on my goals, relinquished my imagination, or quit taking action.

I kept to my task, refused to become negative, held to a positive mental attitude, kept my mind's eye locked on my desire, and practiced effective time-management. Lastly, I hung in there! I knew perseverance would see me through to ultimate success, and it did.

If you are sincere in wanting true success—real wealth, health, and happiness—put these eight success principles to work in your life.

Just one more thing—don't forget to have a thankful heart. We all owe so much to so many others who have helped make this a better world for us. Stop often along the way and say this: "I am thankful for all that I am and all that I will be."

SHEILA L. MURRAY

Sheila L. Murray, author, speaker, trainer, and originator of the Getting Control series is founder and president of Sheila L. Murray Associates, a San Francisco-based business consulting firm.

Sheila is a member of the National Speakers Association, an adjunct faculty member of San Francisco State University, an American Management Association Instructor, and Network Director for the National Association of Female Executives. She is on the advisory boards of The Center For World Business, the Money Lenders, and Studwell Associates of San Francisco.

Sheila has more than 15 years' experience in marketing, sales training, management training, time-management, communication training, and business consulting.

She began her career as coordinator and charter member of an institute for training brain-damaged children. She then went on to a career in the real estate field, distinguishing herself as an award-winning real estate sales person.

Sheila then went back to the personal-development field, this time as an award-winning sales person and manager for a human-growth corporation. She conducted workshops and spoke in cities throughout the country.

In the fall of 1977 she formed Sheila L. Murray Associates, and began a full-time career as a professional speaker-trainer, sharing the platform with the nation's top speakers. Her unique rapport with her audiences has made her one of the fastest-rising stars on the platform today.

Sheila's cassette programs on sales and sales management are being enjoyed and used successfully by men and women throughout North America. Her first book, *Seminaring*, a handbook on the staging and logistics of seminars, workshops, clinics, conferences, and meetings, is due out this year. Her second book, *Getting Control*, is presently being co-authored with William L. Bethel.

You may contact Sheila by writing to Sheila L. Murray Associates, 1390 Market Street, #908, San Francisco, CA 94102 or by telephoning (415) 931-4507.

GETTING CONTROL OF YOUR LIFE

by SHEILA L. MURRAY

A lot of people seem to be concerned about *getting control* these days. I frequently hear people talking about it—*getting control* of their finances, *getting control* of their business matters, *getting control* of their personal lives. Getting control can be a major project.

Somehow, when I hear somebody talking about getting control, I always think about the story of the man who was building a chimney up the side of his house. He stood on the rooftop looking at the dandy chimney he had just built. He was really delighted with it. Then he looked at all the bricks that were left over. He thought, "Gee, I don't want to waste all those bricks. I'll use them to build a barbeque."

He had used a rope-and-pulley system to get the bricks up, so he piled the extra bricks into the bucket, shimmied down the side of the chimney, and untied the rope he had fastened around a tree.

The bucket of bricks weighed more than he did, so to his great surprise, when the bricks started down, he started up. He kept hanging onto the rope, and the bucket met him halfway. It came alongside him and hit him in the stomach.

The man could hardly breathe—he almost passed out—but he held onto the rope and continued on up to the top. When he got there his fingers jammed in the pulley.

About that time the bucket reached the ground. It hit hard, spilling out the bricks. Now the bucket was lighter than the man, so he found himself suddenly on the way down again, and the bucket coming back up. The empty bucket was swinging wildly, and as it passed him it cut him on the forehead. Bleeding and unable to see, he continued on down, hanging onto that rope, and he landed on top of the pile of bricks. He lay there moaning and groaning for awhile, and then he finally let go of the rope.

Now a bucket is heavier than a rope, so the rope started up and the bucket came down and hit him right smack on the head. That's what I call being totally *out of control!*

•

I'd like to share with you three ideas on how to get control of your life so as to live more richly and more fully. They will also help you to avoid "bucket days."

My first tip for you is that eight letters combined spell the most important, most powerful word in our whole vocabulary. Those letters are *A T T I T U D E.*

A key phrase in attitude building goes like this: Attitude makes the major difference in the quality of your life and determines how successful you are. You see, life has two parts. Twenty percent of it is *aptitude*—what you know, your knowledge and your experience. The other eighty percent we call *attitude*. And that's the important part.

I have found out that success is not something you can touch or some place you can go to. Success is an attitude. It's how we feel inside. So today, whether we are successful or not depends on how we feel. I say *today* because we can't affect yesterday—it's gone. And tomorrow isn't here yet. All we have is one day at a time, so we might as well live a rich and full and successful life today.

As I travel around the country talking about attitude building and motivation, people often ask me, "Sheila, are you *really* up all the time—feeling 100 percent good every single day?"

I say, "Well, I'll tell you the truth. About 75 percent of the time I feel pretty good. I've been working on this attitude thing every day for eight years now. But the other 25 percent is like everybody else's—it's called 'bucket days.' I've found out that it isn't humanly possible to be up and feeling wonderful and grand and terrific every single day of your life. It doesn't work that way! Bucket days always come along."

I'd like to share with you my method for handling that. When you wake up in the morning and you can't find your car keys and then, when you do, the car won't start; when no matter what you do, something goes wrong—then you know it's a bucket day.

What I don't do in this situation is dump my bucket of bricks on someone else. What I do instead is say to my colleagues, "This doesn't look like it's going to be my most red-hot day. But if you'll hang in there with me, I'm working on it. My attitude is going to get better."

I've never had anyone say "A bad day, Sheila? What's that?"

What people usually say is, "Boy, do I know what you mean! Let me tell you what happened to me!"

So I think that I have a good attitude about my bad attitude. Maybe, then, I have a good attitude 100 percent of the time!

I think it would be marvelous if we could service our attitudes the way we do our cars. We take the car to the service station, and the attendant checks the oil. Now what if there were a dipstick to tell us when we were a quart low on good attitude, and we could go somewhere to have a quart of it poured into our heads? Wouldn't that solve a lot of our problems?

Do you know anyone who has been around your business a long time, who knows all the answers? This is the person you call when you need to find out how to do something. This person has a lot of aptitude, but often lacks good attitude. If you walk into the office feeling good; if you look out the window and say "Would you look at that gorgeous day!" the expert will glance up and say "Yeah, but look at the dirty windows!"

On the other hand, is there anyone brand new in your business? Someone who doesn't know all there is to know, who has a lot to learn, but is excited and enthusiastic? That person will go charging out the door, try everything, and succeed. Excitement and enthusiasm go a long way.

Another reason for an inexperienced person's success is not knowing that the job is supposed to be difficult. Nobody may have mentioned that!

On a scale of one to ten, how is your attitude today? How do you feel? If you don't like the way your life, or some part of it, is going, the very first thing to check is your attitude.

The second thing I would like to share is something that you know already. You've heard it dozens and dozens of times. It's called planning for the rest of your life, goal-setting and achieving.

Someone once asked me, "Sheila, what is the best time-management course you could give us?"

I said it would be a course in goal-setting and achieving. I believe that we all do what we want to do, and we won't do what we don't want to do.

The key phrase in goal-setting is: It's not what you go after in life that counts; it's what you become along the way. I believe that goals are good for only one thing, what they help us become.

You may already be saying to yourself: "I just know that any minute now she's going to tell me 'You have to write your goals down and you've got to keep them out in front of you!' It sure seems like a lot of work. I don't want to go to all that trouble."

Well, you're right! That's exactly what you have to do! I said the same thing myself about eight years ago: "Gosh, that looks like an awful lot of work! Why would I want to do that?"

I found the answer. There are two kinds of plans in life, yours and somebody else's. I woke up one morning and said "I don't like the way this is working out. Whose plan is this, anyway?" Then I figured it out—*I was following someone else's plan, not mine.*

My question for you is, whose plan are *you* following? Check that one out before the year is up. And in case you haven't done it before or you think you're not too good at it—those things don't matter. Maybe you think you're too old. But even if your hair's a little thin on top, or a little gray, and your posterior spread is greater these days than it used to be, you're never, *never* too old to set goals.

My mother was foreign-born, and the English language was the last of five languages she learned. She thought English was the craziest of them all. One word, like *trunk*, could have half-a-dozen meanings. She decided to get control of the English language, so at age 63 she went to college. Last year, at age 70, she graduated with a degree in English. And five days a week she tutors children with reading problems. She's a dynamic lady, and I can't imagine that she will ever think herself too old for goal-setting and achieving.

I don't know that you can be too young for goal-setting, either. Several years ago I received a call from a high-school principal. He said: "I understand that you do work in the areas of leadership, time-management, goal-setting, self-esteem, and communication. We don't have any money in our budget to pay you, but is there any possible way that you might consider coming down to our school and doing a workshop for our kids?"

I thought that was a tremendous challenge, so I rearranged my schedule and spent five mornings at that school from 9 to 12. I arrived on Monday feeling very much like a teacher. There was a standing lectern, and behind me was a big blackboard, and as all the kids came walking in I felt as if I were about two feet high. They were so big! The very last one to enter the room must have been 6'7". He sauntered in, sat down, stretched his long legs out in front of him, and he seemed to be saying "What's this you're going to tell *us*, lady?" I thought that it was going to be a very long week.

By the time Friday came, I didn't know who had learned more, the kids or I. I called them up one-by-one to give them certificates for completing the course, and when that real tall kid reached out for his handshake, he leaned down and kissed my cheek. It was just great! With all the rest of the kids it was hugs and kisses!

About two weeks later I talked with the basketball coach. He said: "Sheila, what did you do to those kids? They come to the game with a little piece of paper, and they won't tell me what's on it. What's that little piece of paper?"

The goals. It was the list of goals. The principal told me, about a month later, that they had done a locker check, and pasted on the inside of each door were 3 × 5 cards with lifetime goals. He was amazed: "Lifetime goals—and we didn't know that they knew what was going on the day after tomorrow!" Those kids really got turned on.

•

Whether I'm working with school kids or executives, I ask them the same three questions that I'm going to ask you now. They're fun questions to think about, but at the same time they can be heavy, ponderous questions. They can have great significance for your life.

1. What would you like that you don't have? (If you can't answer that question, turn it around and ask yourself what you *have* that you wish you didn't!)

2. What would I like to start that I haven't started? (Now, what do I wish I *hadn't* started?)

3. What would I like to be that I'm not being? (And, of course, what do I wish I were not being?)

You can have a good time with these questions and come up with some entertaining answers. But if life ever becomes difficult for you and you find yourself between a rock and a hard place, get out those questions!

About eight years ago, when I got very serious about attitude building and goal-setting, my life did a flip-flop. I lost my house, my car, and my health. Everything went down the tube, including my attitude.

Someone told me, "Well, Sheila, you have to get good at the goal-setting, and the first thing you need to do is decide what would you like to have that you don't have."

And I said, "I just can't imagine having all those good things back again!"

So my friend turned the question over and asked me "What do you wish you didn't have?"

That was easy for me to answer. Parked outside was a ratty old car. It didn't have any hubcaps, and the ding-strip along the side was gone, leaving all those little holes where it had been fastened. The tip of the antenna was broken off, and the upholstery was all cracked from the sun. I immediately answered "That!"

Then I followed exactly the instructions I was given. I went to every car dealership and looked at cars and sat in cars and moved the seats up and back, and smelled that wonderful new smell that new cars have. I even took a cassette tape with me, and when the salesperson closed the door, I'd play the stereo and try to imagine that that car was mine.

I finally decided on a TR-7. I asked the salesman for five brochures, and I put them up where I would see them over and over during the day. I pasted one on my bathroom mirror, one on the wall next to my desk, and one on my kitchen cabinet. I clipped one to the inside of my briefcase, and I even taped one to the dashboard of the ratty old car. (That's called "Fake it 'til you make it!")

A few months later I took delivery of the TR-7. It wasn't magic, straight and pure, but almost. Seeing my goal over and over every day helped my attitude, and as my good attitude grew and grew, so did my sales and my commissions!

On a Sunday morning I got into that car and went driving down the streets all through town looking at myself in the plate glass windows, hardly believing that I had once again achieved a major goal.

•

The last idea that I would like to share with you is about the most important commodity that we have in life. You cannot buy this on the stock exchange; it's not tradable. This commodity is called *time-management.*

We all want to have enough time to walk all the beaches and climb all the mountains, and we want to have enough time to be successful. There is no way I can teach you how to manage your time in this one chapter, but I can tell you how I learned the value of putting my time to good use. I learned about time-management the hard way.

I have one sister, but I was the boy in my family, my father's son. I was a bit small, and I didn't grow much until I was 15, but I spent a lot of time under the car learning how to change oil. My father had me changing tires by the time I was 12. He wasn't the kind of person who showed his love easily, but I never doubted that he loved me.

My father worked on the railroad for 42 years, and when he retired my mother and he bought a little house out in the country. They were going to do all the things they had always wanted to do.

Not long after, I got a phone call from my father. His voice sounded strangely emotional as he asked me to join him for lunch. That conversation over lunch was the toughest conversation I have ever had in my whole life. We sat there for three-and-a-half hours, while my father took his own inventory—all the things he'd put off doing, that he'd been saving for his retirement. Plans that he and my mother had made.

He told me, "Sheila, you be sure and take those two

young children and do all the things you want to do, because life pulls some very dirty tricks. I just got back from the hospital, and they told me I have six months to live. Sheila, what shall I do?"

I didn't know what to say or do. There was nothing anyone could say or do to make up for all the years that he hadn't carried out his plans, achieved his dreams. Six months later, when my father died, I made a vow: I would make sure that I didn't let my dreams and plans slip by. I would learn to manage my time well. I would even try to do some things he might have enjoyed.

Some years later, while my two sons were still attending high school, I decided that I was going to take them on one heck of a trip. I went to the travel agent and made all the arrangements. I came home with three tickets in my hand and said "Who wants to take a trip?"

Two weeks later we flew up to Canada, landed at Calgary airport, and took a bus up to the Banff-Lake Louise area. We skied for five full days!

The very last morning we were there, we were the first three human beings at the top of a 14,000-ft. mountain. There we were, standing all by ourselves on the top of this mountain with the Continental Divide and the Canadian Rockies all stretched out in front of us! And the sky was the most beautiful clear blue.

It was very cold and it had snowed 4 feet of "powder" the night before. If you are a skier, that much powder makes you think you've died and gone to heaven! My boys came up to me—they are at least 6'2" to my 5'5"—and said "Hey Mom, you want to go first?"

"Sure," I said, "I'll go first."

So I came down the face of the mountain. When I reached the bottom I turned around to look back up, and I couldn't believe it. My two sons were standing there at the top of this huge white mountain. All the pride and joy of my whole life was standing there on top of that mountain!

I waved "C'mon boys!" and my sons came crisscrossing down to me. As they approached, the only sound I could hear was the ssss- ssss- ssss as their skis cut through the snow. And then, with a great yell, they were at the bottom with me.

I took a big breath, and I looked up and said, "How's that, Dad?"

•

Be sure that you don't let either of these two time-wasters get you. One is Ida—boy, if Ida done this, if Ida done that. The other one is Somedayhoney—Somedayhoney we'll do this, Somedayhoney we'll do that. Somedayhoney has destroyed many marriages. Both these time-wasters are terrible. I think we only get one shot at this life, so we might as well make it one heck of a shot!

The theme of everything I do is just one sentence: *Live each day as if your life were being judged by it.*

I try to live that way. I don't succeed all the time, but I try to live each 24-hour chunk so that it contains the essence and the values of my whole life, all the things that are important to me.

I exercise every day. I try to eat the right foods. I try to read every day. I try to have some conversation with The Man Upstairs, I take some quiet time for myself, and I call my mother and tell her I love her.

I have one of those bumper stickers that says "Have you hugged your kids today?" Well, I can't actually hug my kids when they're not home, but when they're away I call them all the time.

If your whole life were being judged by what you do in the 24 hours you have tomorrow, *what would you do tomorrow?*

•

I think the key to getting control and being successful in any career and in your personal life, too, involves one crucial thing. All the courses you take, all the seminars you attend, and all the books you read are a waste unless you do this one special additional thing. *You have to step outside of your daily problems and stretch your hand out to that abyss of poverty that is all around.*

There are all kinds of poverty—financial poverty, educational poverty, spiritual poverty, and physical poverty. If you will help another human being to rise out of that poverty just a little bit, if you will help another human being toward increased pride and dignity—what a wonderful world it can be!

•

I'd like to share with you my very favorite story in the Getting Control series. God sat up in the heavens for eons and eons, and his favorite pastime was throwing lightning bolts down on Earth. They would go crash-bang! crash-bang!

Pretty soon some cave people came out and looked up, and they were very frightened. They ran back into the cave. God didn't care—he just kept on throwing down the lightning bolts.

After a while a little man in a three-cornered hat came out of a little wood house. He was holding a kite. Attached to the kite was a string, and at the end of the string was a key.

God looked down from Heaven, rumbled around among his lightning bolts, and chose an extra big one. He reared back and threw it down, and it went BOOM! It hit the key. Do you know what happened then? That little man lit up the world with electricity!

And God sat up in the heavens and said "I think they finally got it!"

FRANK BASILE

Frank Basile is a successful business executive, educator, lecturer, author and publisher. As an authority in the field of motivation, this dynamic professional speaker relates the techniques and philosophy which have been his own for many years and which have enabled him to achieve success in his business and personal endeavors. He speaks and writes from a depth of personal experience. He has spoken before all types of businesses and organizations from coast to coast on a variety of subjects including personal motivation, time-management, goal-setting, stress and property management. He has written feature articles and monthly columns for many national and regional publications.

Frank was graduated from Tulane University, where he was class valedictorian and student-body president. He then joined the Ford Motor Company to begin a career path which led him to Detroit and then to Indianapolis, where he became the youngest general field manager in the company, with responsibility for the sales and profitability of 175 dealers.

In 1975 Frank made a career change to accept the position of vice president of the Gene Glick Management Corporation, one of the largest and most successful management companies in the country. In this capacity he has responsibility for 18,000 apartment units and 420 employees in 12 states. Frank is a Certified Property Manager (CPM), which is the highest professional designation available in the property management industry. He is also vice president of the National Apartment Association and president of the Apartment Association of Indiana.

He is president of Charisma Publications, Inc., which handles his speaking engagements and the sale of his books. All profits are used for worthwhile civic and community endeavors such as a speech scholarship at Butler University, the Indiana Jaycees, Public Television Station Channel 20, Hooverwood Home for the Aged, the Hedback Community Arts Center, Northeastwood Youth Football Association, Parents Without Partners children's activities, and various senior citizen programs.

Frank serves on the Church Council for All Souls Church and occasionally conducts services and delivers sermons. He is vice president of Indianapolis Free University, vice president of Sales & Marketing Executives of Indianapolis, and a member of the National Speakers Association.

You may contact Frank by writing to him at P.O. Box 40321, Indianapolis, IN 46240 or telephoning him at (317) 844-0719.

COME FLY WITH ME

by FRANK BASILE

I want to share with you my personal feelings about motivation. I may not say anything new or original—you've heard much of it before, perhaps said a little differently. However, since we learn through repetition, perhaps I'll stimulate you to motivate yourself to some desirable action. And, of course, that's where the payoff is.

Nearly everyone wants motivation; many think they have it, but few really do. Motivation is one of the most used and least understood words in the English language. It is not esoteric or mysterious. It is not a big rally or a sales promotion. It is not balloons, a rousing band and a pep talk, or a carrot on a stick, or a whip.

Then what is it anyway?

From a historical standpoint, the first type of motivation known to man was fear. The caveman with the biggest club was the motivator. And, of course, that approach is used to a great extent today. We threaten to fire an employee who does not perform satisfactorily, or we threaten to spank our children if they do not clean their rooms.

The classic example of this type of motivation is the donkey pulling a cart. We've got a whip, and the donkey pulls the cart because of fear of punishment. But because this type of motivation is external, it is only temporary. A person soon becomes immune to it and no longer reacts.

Reward motivation is a little more sophisticated. It is used to a great extent today in the business world. In the model for this type of motivation, the donkey is pulling the cart while chasing a carrot dangling from a stick just out of reach. We have to give the donkey a bite of the carrot after awhile, or it becomes discouraged. But by doing it we destroy the equation—the donkey's not as hungry anymore. Then we need a bigger carrot and a shorter stick, and a lighter load. We find we're paying more and more for less and less. Yesterday's incentives become today's fringe benefits. This type of motivation is also temporary, because it, too, comes from outside the individual.

The only type of motivation that is permanent *comes from within the individual.* It's based on attitude. When we throw away the whip and get rid of the stick and the carrot, we may find out that the donkey is actually a thoroughbred that runs because it wants to. A person performs best because of wanting to, not because of the threat of punishment or the promise of reward.

Motivation = Goal + Plan

Basically, motivation is knowing where we want to go and how we are going to get there. In other words, it is having a goal and a plan. By definition, success presupposes goals. Goals require us to crystallize our thinking, which is sometimes called *introspection.*

Before we can set a goal, we must first understand ourselves, our values, and our priorities. We must know where we are before we can know where we want to go. Socrates gave us the method for understanding ourselves. He said "Know thyself."

We need to ask questions in all areas of our lives— family, social, financial, spiritual, physical, and mental. We will find that these areas are not of equal importance to us, but that in itself is a first step toward establishing our individual priorities. In her book *Grow Up–Not Old* Dorothy Carnegie said, "Life is finding out who you are, learning to *like* who you are, and then learning *to be* who you are." Know yourself, like yourself, and be yourself.

Occasionally I conduct values workshops, in which the participants are asked to list the things they like to do. After one of these workshops, a man told me that as a result of attending one of my previous sessions he had gotten a divorce. He explained that after he had made his list, his wife made one, too. When they compared their values, they found that they had practically nothing in common. Although they had lived together for seven years, they had never discussed where they wanted to go and what they wanted to get out of life. Now they began that long-overdue dialogue, only to determine that they were too far apart to accomplish the things which they individually wanted.

Why this emphasis on goals? Why is goal-setting so important? Because goals give direction to our dreams and help to channel our energy and resources. We could depict our energy, experience, creativity, know-how, and available time as a series of arrows. Without goals, these arrows shoot off in every direction. If we are then able to accomplish anything at all, it is by accident. And probably it is not what we would have chosen had we consciously thought about it.

By contrast, when we have clearly defined goals, there is a clean thrust to our actions. It is like using a giant magnifying glass to focus the sun's rays on a single spot. The resulting intensity can remove obstacles that stand between us and any goal we choose.

It is a generally accepted fact that the average person utilizes only about 15 percent of his potential. Einstein said he used only 10 percent of his. Consider for a moment what you would do with a clock that operated at only 15 percent efficiency. You would probably throw it away. (I'm glad the Lord doesn't feel the same way about us!)

Goals don't increase a person's *potential*, but they increase *percentage utilization*, which is just as important. As a rule, the difference between a disciplined achiever and the average person is not intelligence or native ability, but the *use* to which each person puts those attributes.

We say that knowledge is power. That's not strictly true. *Applied* knowledge is power. Remember the old farmer who was invited to attend a community meeting on new farming techniques? He declined, saying, "I don't farm half as good as I already know how to."

Goal-setting helps us to organize ourselves so that we do not waste time on non-goal-directed activity: Instead of allowing events to control us, we learn how to control them.

•

I carry a 3 × 5 card at all times. Each morning I take about ten minutes to review my goals and see what I can do that day to move toward them. I write down my ideas, and as I accomplish each item I mark it off. This is a most enjoyable time for me. It is motivational in itself, because I know that each action is moving me closer to a goal I consciously chose.

Not too long ago, when I was conducting a workshop on time organization, a lady in the group interrupted to say "I'm glad I'm not like you—running a schedule, everything having to be planned!"

I replied that I like to play and have as much fun as everyone else. I find that if I plan to do the necessary things, I have more time left over to do the things I like.

So often we say we wish we had more time—more time to start a new hobby or read a few more books. We can give ourselves the time to do the things we really want to do if we set goals, prioritize and organize.

John Locke said: "We are born with faculties and powers capable of almost anything such as at least would carry us further than can be easily imagined. But it is only the *exercise* of these powers which gives us ability and skill in anything and leads toward perfection."

Each of us is like an acorn, with the potential to develop into a mighty oak. The way to harness our talents and direct them toward getting the things we want is to know specifically what it is we want and how we can get it. In other words, we need to have clearly defined goals. As Emerson said, "No one ever accomplished anything of consequence without a goal."

A goal works like a guided missile. It's a propellant. We don't want to be like the pilot who announced to his passengers that he had some good news and some bad news: "The bad news is that we are lost; the good news is that we have a 200-mile-per-hour tailwind." Like many of us, he was going nowhere fast. Without goals, we often mistake activity for accomplishment.

The way to harness our power and direct it toward the things we want is to know specifically what it is that we want. That is, we must set specific goals which reflect our values. Goals give direction to our dreams.

•

I have worked with drug addicts, alcoholics and others in need of help. I can say from personal experience that almost any problem, from drug addiction and alcoholism to overeating and loneliness, can be solved to a great extent by goal-setting.

One of the best definitions of happiness that I have ever run across is this: "Happiness is something to do, somebody to love, and something to look forward to." Something to look forward to—that's a goal. If we don't have goals, we're missing a big part of what it takes to get the biggest chunk out of life.

Goal-setting contributes toward happiness in another sense of the word, one which is implicit in this definition by Leo Rosten: "Happiness means using the resources of the mind and heart as deeply and fully as you can."

There was a story in *Time* magazine a few years ago which told about a man who at age 15 had written down all the things he thought he would ever want to do. His list consisted of 157 goals. A few of them were:

- be an Eagle Scout
- type 50 words per minute
- hold my breath under water for 2½ minutes
- read the *Encyclopaedia Britannica*
- sail the South Seas in a schooner

- climb Mt. Everest
- visit every country in the world
- find Noah's ark
- visit the moon

At the time the article was written, the author of that list had just returned from Asia. He had visited three new countries, for a total of 107 countries to date. He had 37 goals to go. This man was disciplined and organized. As a result he was well on his way to realizing all of his dreams.

Quantify Your Goals

During my years with the Ford Motor Company, I found that it was always the same salespeople who were at the top in sales and earnings, year in and year out. They interested me because they were successful due solely to their own efforts.

In January of 1971, shortly after being transferred to the Indianapolis district, I met one of these salespeople. Bill told me that he was going to make about $30,000 that year. That was the income he needed to support his family in the lifestyle they enjoyed. (They had a beautiful home, a swimming pool, and membership in a country club.)

I asked Bill why he was so certain of what he would earn, when a salesperson's earnings are customarily so uncertain and subject to fluctuation.

He replied that to make $30,000 he had to sell approximately 300 new and used cars and trucks during the coming year. (At that point, he had *quantified* his long range goal.)

He went on to state that if he was going to sell 300 cars during the year, he must average 25 cars per month.

He further stated that in order to average 25 car sales per month, he had to sell one car per working day. (Now he had reduced his long-term goal to *short-term goals* which supported it.)

He then reasoned that he could sell approximately one car for every three presentations he made. Good salesmen know their statistics, and he knew that it took him about five phone calls to set up one appointment. Therefore he had to make 15 to 20 phone calls a day to make one sale. (He had now reduced a long-term, relatively uncontrollable goal to a *specific, controllable plan of action.*)

When I went back to that dealership in March of 1972 and asked Bill how things went the previous year, he opened his wallet and took out the W2 form he had been carrying around in anticipation of my visit. His earnings for 1971 were $31,416.21. He had met his goal even though he had taken three weeks of vacation during the year and played golf two afternoons a week whenever weather permitted.

That common thread which distinguishes Bill and all other great salespeople from the average ones is having a goal and a plan. They know where they are going and how they are going to get there.

The Value of Enthusiasm

Once we set our goal, we must decide whether the benefits are worth the price that must be paid. If we are willing to pay what it will cost to overcome the obstacles, then we must create in ourselves a burning desire for the goal. If the potential benefits are not worth the price, then we should discard that goal and move on to another.

Applied desire is really *enthusiasm.* That is the quality that causes us to jump out of bed in the morning with energy and anticipation. Listen to what these men of accomplishment say:

- Disraeli: "The degree of success we achieve depends upon the amount of sincere desire we have."

- Henry Ford: "Nothing worthwhile has ever been accomplished without someone's enthusiasm."

- Emerson: "Every great and commanding moment in the annals of the world is the triumph of someone's enthusiasm."

- Thomas Edison: "When a man dies, if he can pass enthusiasm along to his children he has left them with an estate of incalculable value. It is more than wealth, for enthusiasm will produce wealth—not only wealth, but a great zest for living."

One cardinal principle determines whether a person is successful in selling or anything else: People are persuaded more by the depth of your conviction than by the height of your logic. They may say, "I think, therefore I am;" but their actions say "I feel, therefore I am."

Selling is not converting people to your way of thinking, but rather to your way of feeling. That's why you've got to believe in the product. How can you possibly be enthusiastic about something you don't believe in? You've got to believe what you do and, as a corollary, you've got to do what you believe.

One of my favorite benedictions, which I use whenever I deliver sermons, is from Harry Emerson Fosdick. It goes like this:

Nothing else matters much—not wealth,
nor learning, nor even health—
without this gift: the spiritual capacity
to keep zest in living.

This is the creed of creeds,
the final deposit and distillation
of all of man's important faiths:
that he should believe in life.

The Road Less Traveled

Once when I was on a TV show, the interviewer noted that it was well and good for people to have challenges and set exciting goals as I had described. But then he said, "What's wrong with a man who goes to work each day at the factory or office, comes home every evening at 5:00 p.m., turns on the television, drinks a beer, and watches TV until he's ready to go to bed?"

I replied that there is nothing wrong if that is what the man enjoys doing. Then it's fine. But if he is acting out of his fear of risking change and accepting a challenge, then that's bad. Then he's dead, waiting only to stop breathing before being buried. Henry David Thoreau described this well: "The mass of men lead lives of quiet desperation."

If we are not doing the things that we enjoy doing, there are two possible reasons. One is that we have not taken the time to identify our values and priorities. The second is that we are too busy doing other things.

In either event, we had better take immediate action before it is too late! We must identify those activities and people and things which contribute to our well-being and happiness. Then we must exclude everything else.

In deciding what we want to do or become, the deciding factor should be *what we ourselves choose,* with no consideration of whether it is conventional or reflects the desires and opinions of others. We may not always choose the charted course, but any course is right so long as it reflects our own values and priorities.

The last three lines of Robert Frost's poem "The Road Not Taken" are well worth remembering:

Two roads diverged in a wood, and I—
I took the one less traveled by,
And that has made all the difference.

We all know people who are perpetually turned on. It's exciting to be around them. They are alive and positive. They have goals and challenges in many areas of their lives.

When Mark Twain was asked for the secret of his success, he replied, "I was born excited." At the age of 79, Frank Lloyd Wright built the Guggenheim Museum. When a newspaper reporter asked that innovative architect which of his structures he considered to be his greatest achievement, he responded "The next one!"

The Enemy Is Us

Do you know how to train fleas? Just put them in a glass jar with a top on it. They will continually jump up and down, but they won't be able to go any higher than the lid. After awhile, the fleas will not jump out even when the lid is removed. They will never rise any higher than where the lid used to be. Like most of us, they will be limited by what they think the limits are.

Have you ever wondered how a three-ton elephant can be kept in place by a mere rope and a wooden stake? When that elephant was young, it was chained to an iron stake. No matter how the elephant pulled, it could not get free. Now that the elephant is full grown, it can easily pull up the stake, but it does not try; it has become conditioned by failure.

In most cases we are our own worst enemies. A classic statement in the Pogo comic strip was "We have met the enemy and it is us." It is simple, but true.

On the evening of October 29, 1974, I heard two bulletins on the radio within an hour of one another. One originated in California and concerned a man who almost died following what was supposed to have been a relatively routine operation. The other one, from Africa, had to do with a man who won a prize fight against all expert predictions.

These two events thousands of miles apart had something in common. Each one was clearly related to attitude. The man in California was Richard Nixon—a man whose goals and plans had been shattered, who had nearly lost his will to live. The man in Africa was Muhammad Ali, who had overcome three-to-one odds to regain the heavyweight championship of the world. Ali believed that he was the greatest, and he was. What a great difference attitude can make on our destiny!

I once came across a cartoon that showed a bum sitting on a bench in New York's Central Park with an empty whiskey bottle on the ground nearby. Dressed in shabby clothes, with bloodshot eyes and a forlorn look on his face, the bum was watching a chauffeur-driven limousine as it passed along Park Avenue. In the back seat of that limousine sat a man sipping a drink and reading a newspaper. The caption read: "There, except for me, go I."

Our own attitude of confidence literally determines our capacity. Basically, we set our own limitations. Everyone told Roger Bannister that it was physically impossible for any man to run the mile in four minutes. They said that his heart and stamina could not stand it. But Bannister did not believe them. For months he practiced running and breathing, and he finally achieved his goal. Then, when they saw that it could be done, scores of other runners were able to duplicate his feat.

"Some men see things as they are and say 'Why?' I dream of things that never were and say *'Why not?'* " This quotation from George Bernard Shaw was a favorite of Robert Kennedy's.

An old Chinese proverb says the same thing another way: "Man who say it cannot be done should not interrupt man doing it."

Paying the Price

Desire, when reinforced by confidence and held together by a plan, propels us inevitably toward our goals. With this momentum going for us we are not likely to quit. We will be willing to pay the price.

Winston Churchill did not become Prime Minister until he was 65, when many men have already retired. Prior to that time he had lost numerous elections and experienced many setbacks. Not until after 65 did he achieve the greatness for which we now remember him.

Babe Ruth is known as the great home-run hitter but he also holds the strike-out record.

Henry Ford failed and went broke five times before he finally succeeded.

Here are the words of some other people who understood what it meant to pay the price:

- John D. Rockefeller: "The common denominator for success is work. Without work, man loses his vision, his confidence and his determination to achieve."

- Thomas Edison: "Genius is 99 percent perspiration and 1 percent inspiration."

- Alexander Hamilton: "All the genius I have is the fruit of labor."

- Michelangelo: "If people knew how hard I worked to

get my mastery, it wouldn't seem so wonderful after all."

- Carlyle: "Genius is the capacity for taking infinite pains."

- Paderewski: "Before I was a genius I was a drudge."

James J. Corbett, the famous heavyweight champion of the world, was once asked what it took to be a champion. He replied, "The ability to fight one more round."

•

There is great opportunity in the world today, even with inflation, recession, and continual threat of war. Experience has confirmed for me that every apparent setback or problem carries with it the seed of greater opportunity. In times like this, I am reminded of what Edgar Howe said: "Every successful person I have ever heard of has done the best he could with conditions as he found them, and not waited until next year for better."

The word *crisis* in the Chinese language consists of two symbols—one denotes *danger* and the other denotes *opportunity.*

•

I am going to ask you to set one goal before you go to sleep tonight. It doesn't have to be anything far-reaching. It could be as simple as something you have been thinking about for awhile and never got around to doing. But select just one goal, not a string of New Year's resolutions. Write that goal on a 3 × 5 card. Keep the card in your pocket or purse as a reminder of your goal until it is accomplished. Then set another goal, and continue until goal-setting becomes a habit.

At first, the practice of these success steps will take

deliberate, conscious effort. But before long it will become habitual, and then we will set goals, plan for their accomplishment, create desire, become self-confident, and have determination—all automatically. Success will be a habit. As Emerson said, "We form habits and then our habits form us."

The Success Triangle

Success can be viewed as an equilateral triangle. Skill, knowledge, and attitude are its three equal sides. The amount of happiness or satisfaction or dollars you obtain is dependent upon the interaction of these elements.

To illustrate the success triangle, a salesman might have great enthusiasm (attitude) and know all about the product (knowledge). However, if he doesn't know how to close a sale (skill), his earnings will be severely limited.

By the same token, unless this salesman keeps himself up to date on product knowledge, he will be able to effectively apply only a limited amount of skill and attitude. And if he should have a negative attitude, that would become the limiting factor in his triangle.

When Andrew Carnegie was asked what he considered most important in industry—labor, capital or brains—he replied with a laugh, "Which is the most important leg of a three-legged stool?"

Using Time Effectively

Time is the essence of life. It is our only basic irreplaceable, diminishing resource. How we spend our time determines the quality of our lives. How we spend our time at work determines how productive we are and, therefore, how much we earn. Goal-setting is the most important element of a time-management program. It is impossible to organize our time unless we know what we are organizing to accomplish.

There are numerous time-saving techniques that can boost your effectiveness. Here are a few:

- Commit your goals and timetables to writing.
- Prioritize your activities in order of importance.
- Don't mistake activity for accomplishment.
- Minimize interruptions.
- Generate as little paperwork as possible.
- Don't spend time worrying about what has already happened.
- Do it *NOW*.

I want to emphasize, however, that these can only be effective if we have first defined our goals and priorities. Any activity—church, club, business, marriage—that does not contribute to our happiness is not worth wasting another minute on. Start doing those things which make you happy!

Some friends of mine were talking recently about what they would do if they didn't have to work. One said that if he didn't have to work he would play tennis. Another said that he would learn how to draw. Then he turned to me and said "Frank, what would *you* do if you didn't have to work?" I answered that I would do exactly what I am doing now. If it weren't so, I wouldn't be doing it.

The only way you can be successful at anything is to do it because you *enjoy* doing it. And then you will be not only *successful,* but also *happy.*

•

Here are the four qualities which I feel are most important for maximum achievement and success in any endeavor.

1. *Single-mindedness.* You must know what your goals are and have a strong desire to accomplish them. You must be self-motivated in order to have the determination not to quit when you encounter a setback. When you make mistakes you will learn how to be more effective the next time.

2. *Good organization.* You must develop a step-by-step plan of action to accomplish the goals. Time is your critical resource and it is imperative that it be used fully.

3. *A commitment to hard work.* If the desire is strong enough and the goal is attractive enough, then you will be willing to put in the hours without thinking of it as *work.*

4. *A positive mental attitude.* You must be results-oriented and willing to adjust the plan if it furthers the attainment of the goal. You must be a "possibility thinker," always looking for ways to improve your methods, always willing to listen to and absorb the ideas and suggestions of others.

Success requires a definite goal, a strong desire, and an organized timetable of action. Add determination and a positive mental attitude and you have the basic ingredients for your own success and happiness.

GERARDO JOFFE

Gerardo Joffe is founder and president of Henniker's, one of the best known, most unusual, most innovative, and most successful mail-order houses in the United States.

He was previously the founder and president of Haverhill's, a mail-order house that he started from scratch without any guidance or previous knowledge of the field. Within five years, by pioneering merchandising methods that are now standard procedures in the industry, he developed Haverhill's into what was almost a "national institution." In 1971, he sold Haverhill's to Time, Inc., for more than $1 million.

Despite the author's prominence in the mail-order field, marketing is his second career. A native of Berlin,

Germany, he spent his youth working as an engineer in the tungsten and tin mines of Bolivia and, after coming to the United States, in the oil fields of Texas and Arkansas. In a complete break with the past, he switched to marketing and created his two successful mail-order businesses.

Gerardo Joffe is a professional engineer and a graduate of the Harvard Business School. He lives in San Francisco, is married, and has three children. He is the author of *How You Too Can Make at Least $1 Million (But Probably Much More) In the Mail-Order Business.*

You can contact Gerardo Joffe at Box 7584, San Francisco, CA 94120. Telephone: (415) 433-7540.

MY SECRET SUCCESS FORMULA

by GERARDO JOFFE

I assure you, to describe in a few pages how I became a millionaire is a very large order. First of all, let me tell you about the concept of being a millionaire.

It's kind of imaginary, that magic million dollars that all of us want to obtain. Of late, it has lost much of its glamour—50, 25, or even 10 years ago, a million dollars was a very, very large amount of money. It was so large as to be almost unimaginable for most people. Once you had a million dollars the world was your oyster. You could do anything you wanted to do, and you didn't have a care in the world.

While it's still pretty nice to have a million dollars, it simply isn't what it used to be. But even so, the idea of being a millionaire is still a powerful concept in our society. It's a great touchstone of success—proof to ourselves and to the world around us that we have really made it, that we have achieved the Great American Dream.

I must confess that even I am not entirely immune to this kind of feeling. I remember very well the day when my net worth reached and surpassed that magic million dollar figure. *(It happened in one day!)* Suddenly I thought of myself as a better, more successful and smarter person than I had been the day before.

Obviously, this was nonsense. I was the very same guy I had been before. I still put my pants on one leg at a time; I still ate the same kind of breakfast. My children still didn't mind me. My wife was as skeptical of me as always. My family was not impressed.

I must tell you about a friend of mine, a professional whom I had always thought of, and still think of, as a very fine, very successful person. His net worth always hovered around the $800,000 or $900,000 level. And he had always wanted a million in the worst possible way.

My friend had quite a few holdings in the stock market. And one day when the market was doing well he looked in the paper and saw that he had made $50,000 on paper. He added up all his assets to find that he was worth $975,000—and it drove him crazy.

Later that night he called me. He said, "I thought my home was worth $120,000, but I just talked to the guy down the street, and now I think it's worth $160,000. So I'm worth $1,015,000!"

He was a happy man: his net worth was more than a million dollars—he suddenly was a *millionaire!* He never talked about it again. He's still the same good old guy, but now he has a million dollars and he's happy.

Now, having deflated the whole concept of being a millionaire, let's not talk about that anymore. Let's talk about success and what it takes—at least in my opinion—to be successful.

You are success-oriented. That's why you are reading this. Either you already are a substantial success, or you stand on the threshold of success. Are you impatient? Do you despair because you are already 30 years old, 35 years old, perhaps even 40 years old, and still don't "have it made?" Take heart. Very few fortunes in this country, except perhaps for pop singers' or baseball pitchers', are made at an early age. It takes learning, it takes maturing, and it takes being kicked and buffeted around a little by the "School of Hard Knocks" before you're likely to be a great success.

Take my own case. I was not born in this country. In fact, I came here at age 26. I didn't speak any English and I didn't have a college education. I had no money. And do you know what my profession was? I was a miner. Can you think of a more unlikely beginning for building a great fortune?

I worked in the mines and the oil fields until I was 35, and then I finally decided, at age 35, that a life in the mines and the oil fields was not for me. I realized I would never be able to be anything, become anything, that I would never be able to develop my potential, *if I didn't tear myself loose and start all over again.*

When I made that decision, I had a wife, a child, and absolutely zilch to fall back on. Yet I never regretted making that change, and I never looked back in sorrow for having done it. Why do I tell you this? To show you how great I am? How decisive I am? No, I'm telling you *so that you can take heart.*

You are perhaps younger now than I was then, when I made my big change. And you may have fewer responsibilities than I had then. I threw everything away—a job, a pension plan, security, retirement benefits—because I realized that I was on the wrong track, in the wrong groove. *I was not positioned for success.* If I wanted to be successful I had to pull myself up from what I was doing—not just think about it, but *do something.* To pursue my goal I had to take the very difficult step of making a fundamental change.

It goes without saying that in order to be successful you have to analyze very carefully what you are jumping into, and even after careful analysis, sometimes you may go wrong. I went from the mines to the mail-order business. Nothing I had ever done before had prepared me for this kind of career.

Why did I choose the mail-order business? Was it luck? Was it serendipity? Did anybody take me by the hand and guide me? Did anybody suggest it to me? No! What I did was to take stock of my assets, my talents, and what I wanted to do. I tried to locate a field of activity that best suited all three.

Here are the talents I found I had: I had a knack for advertising and promotion. I had an understanding of business organization. (I had read about that.) I had a talent for copywriting, and I knew I was a good writer. I had a knowledge of languages. I had knocked around on two or three continents, and was at home in at least three or four languages. And ever since childhood, I had had a knack for numbers. I can do things with numbers in my head.

So I looked at all possible careers, and at many possible businesses. It gradually became clear to me that I would be able to use these talents best in the mail-order business. And further, that I should be in that branch of the mail-order business that dealt with technical merchandise. That would be the area where my engineering and mechanical background would serve me best. It was a good choice. I was successful. I was so successful that in five years I achieved my secret dream and became a millionaire.

I was successful because *I had positioned myself* in something I could do well and for which I had talent. I was successful because I chose an industry that was bound to grow and grow. And I was successful because I worked as hard as I knew how. Finally, I was successful because I took risks with myself and I took risks with money.

Are you doing what you are best suited for? Or are you a round peg in a square hole? Well if you are a round peg in a square hole, if you are in the wrong spot, *get out now!* I did it, and you can, too.

If you are in the wrong spot, stop fretting. Just set your eye on what you want to do and take the decisive step. Conversely, if you like what you're doing and if you are doing what you are talented for, you will be doing it well and you are bound to be successful.

The next success point is: Are you in a business that is growing? Or are you still tied to a business like making buggywhips? There is a vast selection of businesses that express the lifestyle of tomorrow and the opportunities of tomorrow for you to choose from. Many of them are businesses and industries unheard of even five years ago. Pick one that is suited to your talents and it will be a step toward success.

Are you willing to work hard? I tell you, *don't let them kid you!* There is no lazy way to riches. For real success, perhaps even your spouse and your kids will have to work hard. Later, while you drive your fancy convertible or Italian sports car, or sit in your new condominium or ski chalet, then you can think back on all the hard work done by you and yours. But I assure you, you cannot sit on your fanny and be successful. You've got to go out there and hustle! You show me someone who claims to have become a millionaire by being lazy, and I'll show you a person who inherited a million dollars, married a million dollars, or is a liar.

The last reason I give for my success has to do with taking risks and being able to invest money. This is perhaps the most difficult to talk about, because the other three were somewhat self-evident. You must look very carefully before you risk your money, *but you must risk.* You must be willing to take a prudent gamble. Don't be afraid to lose money. Make up your mind that if you do shoot the works, or part of it, you can start all over again.

Of course it's tricky to define just what a prudent gamble is. It isn't always the one that succeeds. Even if you lose, if you look back and say "Darn it, I lost it, but it was a good shot!"—that was a prudent gamble. But I have to tell you, you don't gamble or risk just once, when you make that initial investment or when you buy that franchise. No—you have to gamble *all along the way,* even when you are at the very top. Therefore, an important ingredient for success is to be willing to take risks with your money, risks commensurate with the capital you have.

Naturally, at first the risks you take will be fairly small. But as you go along they will be larger. At every step of the way you must continue to develop the ability to distinguish between the prudent gamble (even if it does not ultimately succeed), and the crazy "crap shot" (even if it does).

So there you have it. What do you have to do to become a millionaire? My own formula is this: *Get into something for which you have talent, get into a growth business, work hard, and take risks.*

There is actually more to success than that formula. There are certain personal qualities that you must have. I believe there are absolutely *indispensable* personal qualities for reaching success—for becoming a millionaire, if you wish. Obviously, one of these is the willingness to work hard. Nothing is going to be handed to you on a silver platter, but we have already talked about hard work, so we won't mention that again.

Another one of these qualities is that you have to be smart. And I don't mean "school smart." You don't have to know the sequence of the kings of England. You don't have to know spherical geometry. But you do have to be able to see opportunities, to assess risks in relationship to possible rewards. You have to be able to weigh consequences. You have to know how to handle yourself even if you fail. You have to have savvy. You have to be "life smart."

You also have to have faith and confidence in yourself and in your own abilities, while understanding your limitations. Blind faith, with no consideration of your limitations, can make you look foolish instead of successful.

There are many successful people in this world who are limited. They are successful because they know where their limitations lie, and they are willing and able to delegate those areas to others.

The road to success is not at all smooth. I assure you that there will be many pressures and reversals along the way. If you cannot take the licks, and if you cannot pick yourself up, you cannot be a success. I know it sounds a little corny, but Harry Truman used to say "If you can't stand the heat, get out of the kitchen."

And I tell you, get out of the millionaire's race, if you cannot stand the heat of pressures, reverses, and temporary defeats!

Finally we come to the requirement which may be the most important one for personal success—the ability to get along with people. Nothing that you do on your road to success will be done in a back room or up in some ivory tower. You will be working *with people and through people.* And you can't do that by cracking the whip. You have to make people like you, respect you and want to work with you.

If you realize that you have a little trouble in that area, I'll give you some really good advice: Spend every effort to remedy that flaw. *Learn how to get along with people now,* because I assure you that you cannot be successful if you don't learn that.

Now I've given you my "secret formula!" I'm just one guy here telling you what *he* believes are the most important points in pursuing success. But they have worked for me. I think they will work for you.

I would like to say a few last words about my business, the mail-order business. I think it is absolutely the greatest business in the world, and "we ain't seen nothin' yet!" Right now it's a $50 billion industry and it's growing and growing. I invite you to join me in this great business. We need people like you—success-oriented people, people who are ambitious and want to make a million dollars. I assure you that this is a business in which you *can* make a million dollars.

But don't let anybody kid you about the mail-order business. Not everyone can do it. It isn't that easy. You have to learn. You must read and study before you can expect to be successful at it. If you have the personal qualities for success that we have just been talking about, and if your talent inventory shows that you are suited for any phase of this business, you have an excellent chance for success. And who knows? You may be a millionaire just five years from now! Then you will write *your* "secret formula," so others can see how it's done. Nothing could please me more than that.

DAVE GRANT

Dave Grant is the president of Dave Grant Productions, which produces educational films, cassettes,and seminars. He is the author of three books, *Heavy Questions*, *Compass for Conscience*, and *You've Got What It Takes.*

One film by Dave Grant Productions,"The Well-Rounded Square," received a first-place award from the Freedoms Foundation at Valley Forge and was purchased by the U.S. Army for moral and character guidance classes.

A well-traveled lecturer, Dave Grant presents more than 100 seminars a year to executive, management, and sales personnel. He makes another 100 presentations yearly as featured speaker for organizations across the nation and in 19 other countries.

A graduate of Bob Jones University in Greenville, South Carolina, Grant has lived for the past 29 years in California. He is an active member of the National Speakers Association, the Sales and Marketing Executives of Los Angeles, and the Los Angeles Chamber of Commerce. He is listed in *Who's Who in the West*.

You may contact Dave Grant by writing to him at P.O. Box 273, Encino, CA 91436; or by telephoning (213) 986-9166.

I AM SOMEBODY
BECAUSE . . .

by DAVE GRANT

How many times have you heard a salesperson ask the question "I wonder why I have so many ding-a-ling clients?" You may not like the answer, but I'm going to give it to you anyway! *Radiation equals attraction.* Whatever we radiate, we attract.

I did a seminar the other day for the service department of a car dealership. The mechanics were very talented, well-trained, and efficient. There was no concern about their ability, but their basic premise was "Everybody who drives in here is trying to rip us off—but *we're* going to get *them* first!"

That's what they were radiating. Now what do you think they were attracting?

All we had to do to improve this shop's performance was to turn the attitude around. We showed those mechanics how to operate with a new thought in mind: "Everyone who drives in here is a beautiful person with real needs that we can meet better than anybody else—*and we're going to be friends for life!*

Now what did they radiate, and what did they attract? I got a letter from the manager weeks later. He said, "We've had hardly a single complaint on the driveway since you were here, and I really like that."

•

What kind of clients do you have? They're just like you. If you don't like your clients, *change who you are!* You see in people what you see in yourself. That's what you're radiating; that's what you're selling. You're selling yourself, and I want you to fall madly in love with your product!

The other day a lady in Bakersfield asked me, "David, how can I love myself with all of my faults?"

We've all wondered that at some time or other. The answer, of course, is that if I can't love myself with all of *my* faults, how am I going to love you with all of *yours?* I can't. I can't love you and accept you any more than I love and accept myself.

If I love and accept myself, what do I radiate? Love and acceptance. What do I attract? Love and acceptance. It's natural.

If I don't love myself, that's rejection, a form of self-hate. If I don't love myself I radiate anger, bitterness, resentment, and revenge. What do I attract? Those same things. I attract rejection, and I end up asking "I wonder why nobody likes me?"

We all want to be accepted by people. We want people to feel good about us, to like us. To achieve that we must learn to love ourselves. And to do that *we have to make the distinction between who we are and what we do.*

One way to find out who you are is to use comparison. To begin, compare yourself to things. Are people, are you, as valuable as things?

Suppose your spouse comes home with a huge dent in the side of the car. What do you respond to first, the person or the dent? If you respond to the dent first, what are you saying? "Things are more important and valuable to me than people."

Several months ago my wife received as a gift a piece of Irish china called Belleek, handmade and very fine. As a rule we put things to use at our house, because that's what things are for, to be used. We were using this pitcher—that is, our eight-year-old was. She had just refilled it with milk and was returning to the table in her stocking feet on a waxed floor . . .

Well, she didn't make it. As she started to sit down, her feet went out from under her, and the pitcher crashed onto the table, breaking into a thousand pieces. She hung onto the handle, though, and as I reached out to help her she raked it right across my forearm, laying open the flesh. Then she landed flat on the floor, sprawled out amongst milk, china, and blood.

What do you do in that moment? Is there any way you can compare the value of that china to the value of that child? What is the china worth? A thousand dollars? Five thousand? Do you say "You dumb, stupid, clumsy, irresponsible kid—you broke an irreplaceable heirloom?"

If you do that, what are you teaching that kid? She thinks: "Boy, I wish I were a pitcher, or a vase, or a lamp. I'd get more tender loving care. My parents don't yell and scream like that when *I* get busted!"

Very early in life she learns that things are where it's

at. You go into business to make money, and you use people to make money—people don't count.

When you equate people with things, objects, it's easy to consider them in terms of dollars. At a realty board meeting not too long ago, a guy drew an arc on his placemat at the table, saying: "New salespeople go into business and they have this nice, beautiful, gradual up-curve for a couple of years—like this. Then they run out of gas—like this. If you can tell me what causes that and how to stop it, you've got some business."

I said "I've got your business. The reason their performance drops off is that they went into business to make money, and they can't be trusted."

Now a lot of people go into business to make money, and they're not going to make it, because they're going at it backwards. They've got the wrong idea.

Let's say that I'm doing the selling and you're the client. *I've got to make a sale!* My rent is due, I've got payments to think about, I've got mouths to feed. I've *got to sell somebody something!* Whose best interest do I have at heart? My own. And who's going to get the better end of the deal? You or me? I am, and you know it!

Can you trust me? No way. Can we make a deal? Not likely, unless I twist your arm, frighten you, or coerce you. And how many times can I do that? Just once.

You don't make money this way. *The secret to making money is meeting people's needs.*

Now before we go any further, I want to give you two definitions, one for success and the other for love. *Success is the ability to establish long-lasting relationships with other people. Love is the commitment of my will to meet your needs, your basic interests, regardless of how I feel.* We establish long-lasting relationships with others in the same way, whether we are talking about a personal relationship or a professional one. And we do that *by put-*

ting their needs and their interests ahead of our own.

Let me try to illustrate what I mean. How would you know that I really cared for you? You would know that I cared for you only if I put your needs and interests ahead of mine. Now—I'm willing to do that for you. *Just as soon as you do it for me!* Does that sound familiar? Does that give you any clue as to why we may not have very many long-lasting relationships? We know what it takes, *we just don't want to go first!*

Let's look at the relationship between a salesperson and a client. To establish a long-lasting relationship, someone *has to move first.* Someone has to put the needs of the other person first. And who is it? In this relationship, who goes first? The salesperson. The salesperson meets the client's needs first.

Are you going to be a success as a salesperson if you say: "Hey, I really need you to buy something from me! Make me a success"?

A few weeks ago I spent some time with an estate planner, and he showed me a dozen plans he could have sold me for my estate. Which of them do you think he wanted to sell me? Most people guess the most expensive one. The layman thinks salespeople are in it for what they can get out of it. Those are the salespeople who aren't in business anymore, but the client doesn't know that.

Twelve years ago an insurance man sold me an estate plan. It was an expensive program. It met his needs—he got a great big commission right up front, right off the top. And he had my business for only one year, while he might have had it for twelve. If that insurance man had met my needs twelve years ago, I would have been meeting his for the past twelve. He sacrificed the permanent on the altar of the immediate.

The worst salesperson in the world is a hungry one.

Can clients tell when a salesperson is hungry? Sure they can, and they know they can't trust you.

I don't know how many times I've had people tell me that they can't sell. Finally they decide to quit, and once the pressure is off, they sell like crazy. All of a sudden they aren't out there to meet their own needs. They're doing it for the fun of it, and all of a sudden something happens between two people, and there's a sale.

Do other people need me? What's the difference if I go out today believing that everybody I meet needs me, or if I go out believing *that I need everybody I meet*? Do you see the difference?

I was talking to a sales group recently and I told them to go out believing "Everybody I meet today needs me. They love me, they trust me, and they believe what I tell them."

When I finished, one fellow said, "That's when you zap 'em!"

Have you ever been zapped? Have you ever been zapped by the same person twice? If you're zapping people, you're working too hard. You've got to keep finding new people to zap.

If I'm a salesman and you're my client, I don't want your business once—*I want your business for life!* It's my responsibility to give you the full 100 percent, to meet your needs 100 percent regardless of what you do or don't do. I've got to be committed to just that.

•

Our house in Encino was too small for our family. For six months we vacillated between selling it and buying a bigger one or keeping it and adding on. We finally decided the neatest, simplest thing was to sell. With that decision in mind I called a realtor. I said "We want to sell our house and buy another one; come talk to us."

So the realtor came to our home one Saturday morning, and he sat down with us for about an hour, I suppose. He asked a lot of questions and wrote a lot of things down on a yellow legal pad. At last he said, and I can almost quote him verbatim, "I'd really like to have your listing, but I think you ought to stay here and add on."

Now if you're hungry, you can't say that. Most salespeople would have walked in there and said *"Give me your listing*—now, let's talk about your needs."

That realtor made a strong effort that day to meet my needs, not his. He did meet my needs, and he didn't make a nickel that day. However, word gets around. If you're zapping people, word gets around. If you're meeting people's needs, word gets around. That's reputation.

•

In the relationship between manager and salesperson, who goes first and meets the needs of the other? If I'm a manager I want to be a good manager. And the best way for me to do that is to develop excellent salespeople. If I build excellent salespeople and meet their needs, they're going to make me look like a million dollars. I've got to go first.

Personally, I know that I would not produce for a manager who didn't care about me and was using me just to get overrides. But if I know that manager will do anything in his power to make me a success, I'll give him my life.

Between owner and manager, who goes first, who initiates? The owner.

Between teacher and student, who initiates? The teacher.

Between parent and child, who meets whose needs first?

Somebody once asked me: "Did you get married to be

a husband, or because you needed a wife? Did you have children because you wanted to be a father, or because you wanted children?" I haven't answered that one yet!

•

Let me ask you another question that will help determine your personal value. Do you consider yourself to be as valuable as an animal?

A fellow was driving down the freeway the other day pulling a horse trailer. He had a horse in there that was worth about 25 grand. He was uptight—tense, nervous, gripping the wheel, knuckles white, perspiration pouring down his face. He told the friend who was riding along, "I've never driven anything this valuable before."

With an incredulous look on his face, the friend said "Man, I've been in your car many times and you're never this careful!"

Have you ever watched a family driving down the freeway? With just themselves, with just their kids? They take all sorts of chances. But when they're pulling a boat, or a trailer, or a camper, then they're super careful, because of the "enormous investment."

What if I were to give you a dog? Not just any dog, but a valuable, purebred, registered AKC dog that cost me $1,000? That's a lot of dog!

Suppose that I give you this dog to take care of for the next 30 days, and while you're taking care of it, I want you to be very, very aware of how valuable it is.

Now how do you suppose you would take care of that dog? Would you see that it ate regularly? Would you shove its head down in the bowl and say: "Come on, hurry up and eat—haven't got time! Better still, bring it with you?"

Would you see that the dog got a balanced diet, or would you let it eat anything it liked, especially if it whined? Would you see that it got proper rest, or would you let it stay up as late as it liked watching television?

Would you exercise that dog regularly, or would you let it get fat and lazy? (What happens to the value of a dog when it's overweight?) Would you keep it up all night at wild parties? Wake it up in the morning with a cup of black coffee and a cigarette: "Come on, Fido, let's go! Come on, wake it up, move it out—get the old adrenalin going"?

Nobody who loved a dog would treat it that way. If we treated dogs the way we treat ourselves, they would never survive! Now, again, consider the question "Are you as valuable as an animal?" Look at how you've treated yourself for the past 30 days and you've got your answer.

•

Do you ever try to dehumanize people? I once did a seminar for a police department, and they spent half the morning trying to define what a human being is. It bothered me for awhile. Then it finally dawned on me that if you're in a war you've got to convince yourself that everybody on the other side is a rat. You can shoot rats all day and go home and sleep at night. But you can't shoot humans. So you rationalize; you dehumanize.

You can't walk away from a human being, either. You have to dehumanize the other person in order to break a relationship: "He's a rat, the way he treated me; I don't know what I ever saw in him." Then you can walk away. We dehumanize in order to justify our failure to relate.

•

How would you compare people to people? It is estimated that by the time we are ten years old, 99.9 percent of us have an inferiority complex. That is not to say that 99.9 percent of us *are* inferior, only that *we feel* inferior. An epidemic of inferiority is raging throughout our society. From the moment children enter the world they are subject to an unjust value system which reserves respect and esteem for only a select few. And those who fail to measure up to society's standards are left to cope with feelings of inadequacy.

An inferiority complex begins with making a comparison between oneself and others. The comparison can be in one or more of these areas: how we look, what we know, and what we have done.

If you don't think looks are important in our society, imagine taking all the "beautiful people" out of the commercials. You don't usually sell things with plain or homely people. Looks count in our society!

What's the best compliment anybody could give you? Does it have to do with your appearance? People get very involved with their eyes, their figures, their beauty. That's O.K., but does that make them "somebody"?

Our society also says you are somebody because of what you know. The more you know, the more you are. If you have a Ph.D., that's the top of the pile. If I have an I.Q. of 100 and you have an I.Q. of 120, you're 20 points "better" than I.

What can I do about that? Well, I could do everything in my power to raise my I.Q. to 120 and be just as good as you. Or I could do everything in my power to make you look stupid. Which is easier?

There are two basic ways in which we relate to people—we build them up or we tear them down. And every time we tear someone down, we are actually saying "I feel inferior." If I love myself I build people. If I don't love myself, I tear people down.

Anytime I've had to say anything bad about someone

I've had to do it to bring that person down to my level. What have I said about myself in doing that? "I feel I'm not as good as . . ." Have you ever heard anyone say that? But how often do you hear someone say "I'm just as good as anybody else?"

Whenever somebody says "I'm as good as . . ." nobody believes it, including the person who said it.

Does a handsome man or a homely one say "I'm as good as . . ."? Does a smart person or a dull one say "I'm as good as . . ."? You see—the minute I say "I'm as good as" all I've done is admit I don't feel that I am.

Often how intelligent we feel depends on who we are with. If I know more than you, I'm obviously smart. If I don't know as much as you, I must be dumb. I try to find out who I am by comparing myself with you, and actually, that doesn't tell me a thing.

•

Another way society judges us is by what we've done. The more we've done, the more we are; the less we've done, the less we are. If you have children, could you describe them right now without mentioning what they've done—or how they look, or what they know? What you have left when you've eliminated those three things is all that really matters.

In order to establish and maintain high self-esteem we must understand the difference between *being* and *doing,* or between *personage* and *performance.*

I heard on the news that an 11¢ airmail stamp had just been auctioned off for $35,000 because the airplane on it was printed upside down. That stamp was unique. It was one of a kind. In rolls of 100 it would be worth 11¢. But by itself it's special and valuable. And we are all special and valuable.

Remember that lady who asked "How can I love myself? How can I accept myself with all of my faults?" You can accept yourself with all your faults because you are valuable and unique, even with those faults. *There is a difference between who you are and the mistakes you make.* There is a difference between being and doing.

•

I have four children. Why are they mine? They are mine because they were born into my family—that's who they are. What if a child makes straight *A*'s or straight *F*'s—what does that have to do with who that child is? Nothing.

What if a child is quarterback on the football team or waterboy on the end of the bench? Does either have anything to do with who that child is? No.

That kid could spit in my face and swear at my name and I'd work on his performance. But that would have absolutely nothing to do with who that kid is.

I want my child to know "There is never anything you can do to change your position with me. There is nothing so good or so bad that it would ever change my love for you or my acceptance of you."

At the divine, creative level I have been loved and accepted for who I am. Is my relationship with my Heavenly Father determined by my performance, or my looks, or what I know? No—I've been totally loved and totally accepted for *who I am as I am.* My position is safe. It's secure. Now I'm free to perform.

I can accept myself with all my faults because somebody's already done it. And when I can accept myself with all my faults I am free to love and accept you for how you are, as you are.

If you don't know the difference between being and doing, how are you going to love a man because he's your father and hate the fact that he drinks too much? You can't.

What's the difference between saying to a child "You stupid kid!" and saying "You're a smart kid—you ought to know better than to do that stupid thing?" Most of us got the "stupid kid" treatment when we were children, and we grew up thinking that we were stupid. So we did stupid things just to prove it.

What's the difference between telling a subordinate "You idiot!" and "Hey, that wasn't the smartest thing to do?" Is there any difference? There's a world of difference. I can fire someone for what they do, but there's no way I could fire someone for who they are.

•

Several years ago we lived in a house that had a back yard just loaded with flowers. We had all kinds of flowers. The children used to decorate palm trees and doll houses with flowers. They used to take flowers down the cul-de-sac and try to sell them to the neighbors. That was O.K.

But we also had some very special, prize roses in the front yard, and the children were not allowed to pick them. We told them: "Don't touch those roses unless there is somebody there to help you clip them properly or you're going to get paddled. Leave them alone!"

So what did I do when my four-year-old walked in with her hand behind her back singing "Happy Birthday?" "Close your eyes, Daddy, I've got a surprise," she said.

So I closed my eyes and she gave me a handful of beautiful rosebuds ripped off at the base. "I love you, Daddy," she said.

Now I had a problem. I don't think it's possible to deal with that situation without understanding the difference between the person and the performance. I took her in my arms and I said: "Honey, I love you too, You're a very special little girl. I'm glad for you. I appreciate you. Thank you for remembering my birthday."

And then I said: "You did something I told you not to do, didn't you? What did I say I'd do if you did that?"

I paddled her. I had to, for her sake. But I did the very best I could to establish for her *who she was* before I corrected *what she did*. She knew the difference.

You see, the more I love you, the more I can deal with what you are doing that is wrong. The more I love you as a person, the more I'm going to hate that alcohol you are putting into your body.

If you started today to look at your spouse and act toward your spouse as if that person were perfect, what do you think would happen? What do you suppose would happen if you did that for six months?

Pay close attention to these words of Goethe: "If I treat you as you are, you will remain as you are. If I treat you *as if you were what you could be,* that is what you will become."

Most of us react to a person's negativism and reinforce it: "That's just like you—you did it again! I don't know why you keep doing it; you know how much it bugs me!"

What if, instead, you reacted every time that person did something good, creative, beautiful? What if you said "That's just like you to do such a beautiful thing"?

I remember a couple who came to my office with real problems. They were trying to solve them in the usual way, he trying to change her, and she trying to change him. At one point he said "I would really love for her to read books." And he listed some. "And," he added, "I wish she'd go to all these seminars that I go to. And listen to all those tapes I want her to hear . . ."

I asked him why he wanted his wife to do all those things.

"Because I know what a wonderful woman she could be," he replied.

Now what kind of message do you think his wife got from that? Clearly, it was: "I don't love you as you are— but if you'll do these things, if you'll perform all these ways and become the person I want you to, *then* I'll love you."

That's what most of us say, "Meet my standards. The more you perform, the more I'll love you. The less you perform, the less I'll love you. I'll love you as soon as . . ."

What is love, again? *The commitment of my will to meet your needs and interests regardless of how I feel.*

Think of the most loving thing you ever did. Was it easy or hard? When asked what she liked best about herself, one lady answered "my compassion for nice people." Now would you say that was easy or hard? Isn't it pretty easy to have compassion for nice people? How about a little compassion for un-nice people?

What does real love do? Real love loves the unlovely as if it were lovely, and thereby it *becomes* lovely.

What if you loved me because of my beautiful face and I were in an accident? What if you loved me because of my mind and I made mistakes? What if you loved me because of what I do and I couldn't do it anymore? That kind of love is always insecure.

Then there's the love that says "I love you for who you are, as you are. Unconditionally. Don't ask me *why I love you*, ask me *if I love you*. Why is a condition, and there are no conditions."

A man said to me, "Dave, if I did that I'd be intellectually dishonest."

What he really meant was that he'd be emotionally dishonest. That wasn't what he was feeling, so how could he treat her that way? What is love? The commitment of will—not feelings, but will.

C. S. Lewis said "If I knew I loved my neighbor, how would I treat him? Having determined that, treat him that way, regardless of how you feel."

Don Quixote had a lady in his life who was known as a woman of the streets, but he always referred to her as "my lady." Years after their ways parted, when he was on his deathbed, she came back to visit him. She was different. He barely recognized her. She had to tell him who she was: "I'm your queen."

Because Don Quixote treated Dulcinea, with all her faults, as if she were a lady, a queen, that's what she became. That's what love is all about.

Treat your wife as if she were a queen, and she'll become a queen. Treat your husband as if he were a king, and he'll become a king.

When I suggested to one group that for six months they treat their spouses as if they were perfect, one man said to me "If I did that for six months, she'd be looking for a new man."

I said "Try it for six months and *you'll be a new man!*"

•

People ask me all the time, "David, what do you think makes *you* somebody?"

My favorite answer is "I am somebody because I am *loved,* I am *accepted,* I am *forgiven,* and I am *free.*" And they all mean the same thing.

JERRY V. TEPLITZ

Jerry V. Teplitz is a graduate of Hunter College and Northwestern University School of Law. Formerly an attorney with the Illinois Environmental Protection Agency, Mr. Teplitz is currently a certified consultant for Performax Systems International, Inc., the president of his own consulting firm, and the holder of the title Master Teacher of Hatha Yoga from the Temple of Kriya Yoga.

During the past five years he has lectured to more than 100,000 participants on a program titled "Managing Your Stress: How to Relax and Enjoy."

Mr. Teplitz has been employed as a management consultant for Executive Systems, Inc., and has served as a staff trainer for Consultants in Planned Change.

In his position as a certified consultant for Performax Systems International, Inc., he specializes in self-administered instrumentation programs aimed at increasing employee productivity and efficiency. His own consulting firm conducts seminars, lectures, and workshops for businesses, schools, and conventions in the area of stress management and employee productivity.

Mr. Teplitz is the author of the book *How to Relax and Enjoy . . .* , and he is presently writing a book related to executive and office stress.

He has appeared on numerous radio and television shows throughout the United States and Canada to demonstrate a variety of stress-reduction techniques. Articles about Mr. Teplitz have appeared in local and nationally syndicated newspapers and magazines, including a featured interview in *Prevention* magazine.

Mr. Teplitz is a member of the National Speakers Association. You can contact him by writing 214 78th Street, Virginia Beach, VA 23451 or telephoning (804) 428-1628.

MANAGING STRESS

by JERRY V. TEPLITZ

The stresses of life are all around us. According to Han Selye, M.D., there are good stresses and bad stresses. Good stress is caused by joyous events—for example, the birth of a child or advancement in one's work. Bad stress results from the loss of a job or a loved one; on a smaller scale, it occurs many times every day.

All change causes stress. Stress is basically the demand that one adapt to a new situation with different responsibilities. Our modern society exposes us to extremely rapid changes in almost every area of life, and the human organism is continually in the process of adapting.

Stress is manifested in many ways. More than 35

million people in this country have hypertension, and about 20 million are alcoholics. We spend more than $75 billion yearly on health care.

Stress has a major economic impact at the business level. Replacing executives who suffer from heart disease costs more than $900 million yearly. Statistics show that 35% of all deaths are due to myocardial infarctions, and an additional 11% are due to strokes. While these figures have been decreasing in very recent years, the levels are still threateningly high.

An estimated 5% to 8% of the nation's executives are alcoholics and cost their organizations an average of $4,000 per individual each year in lost time, waste, and inefficiency. An anxiety-prone employee can cost a company $3,700 per year.

Overall, the annual financial cost of troubled employees in terms of sick leave, alcohol-related deficiencies, inattention to job, and waste is estimated to exceed $60 billion. This does not even take into account the damaging effects on personal relationships in the office and at home.

Unfortunately, the stresses of work and home life tend to build on each other. A glance at the divorce rate, currently about 50%, reveals a tremendous amount of stress which either stems from or is expressed in the marital relationship.

While this picture is discouraging, there is no need for you to experience the tolls which stress exacts. You have the power to take charge and change your reaction to the stresses in your life. *Your mind and body have almost unlimited power to alter the way in which everything in your environment is affecting you.*

In our Western culture we are systematically trained *not* to use these internal powers. For this reason most people feel stuck with their attitudes. They are unaware that it is possible to change them. Changing your attitudes so that you no longer react to things that would ordinarily trigger emotions can reshape your life. In fact, *just making a decision to change* can have a tremendous impact on one's life.

Using Mind Power

A very powerful tool developed by John Diamond, M.D., will allow us to understand and utilize our internal powers. Diamond calls it *behavioral kinesiology.* I call it *body talk.*

Body talk is based on the concept that everyone and everything in our external and internal environment measurably affects us. Dr. Diamond says that it is possible to immediately determine these effects by testing muscle resistance. We can use this test to demonstrate that the power of positive thinking is not just an idea— that it has obvious physical effects. This test requires a partner.

Instructions:

1. Your partner faces you with one arm at the side of the body and the other arm raised out until it is at a 90° angle to the floor, thumb pointing toward the floor.

2. Place one of your hands just above your partner's wrist on the extended arm. Place your other hand on your partner's opposite shoulder. *(See Figure 1.)*

3. Instruct your partner to resist as you push down on the extended arm. You are not trying to force the arm down; you simply need to feel the normal level of resistance. Push with a steady pressure for several seconds; then release.

Figure 1

4. Keeping the same position, arm extended, your partner should think of something sad or someone disliked. Allow a few seconds for focusing on the thought. Then push down on the extended arm. It will usually go down easily, though your partner resists.

5. Wait a few seconds, then tell your partner to resume the position while thinking of something gratifying or someone well liked. Again, allow a few seconds for focusing on that image, then push down on the arm. The arm will usually stay level and strong, even if you push harder than before.

•

You have just discovered the power of the mind. When a person is envisioning something sad, painful, or disliked, the arm will test weak; it will not resist your pushing. A happy thought will keep the person's internal energies strong, and the arm will test strong.

Switch roles and have yourself tested by your partner. You may be skeptical at first and find yourself focusing on resisting the pressure on your arm. But when you honestly concentrate on a negative image, your arm will go down easily.

This simple test clearly illustrates the process that takes place within us whenever we dwell on negative thoughts. A person who continually holds negative thoughts or emotions in mind will eventually become ill. The life energies will have weakened so much that the body's resistance to disease will be seriously impaired.

Similarly, negative thoughts or reactions throughout the day can wear down your body's resistance to stress. This is a reinforcing cycle: the more stress you feel, the more discouraged, frustrated, angry, and tense thoughts you have; and the more negative thoughts you have, the more susceptible and sensitive you are to stress. At the end of the workday you find yourself tired, irritable, and functioning at a low energy level.

Now there are many things you can do to break the stress cycle and keep it from controlling you. One technique utilizes part of what you learned in the preceding test: when you think a positive thought, your energy stays strong and your arm does not go down.

During the day, when you are thinking negatively or are under a great deal of stress, close your eyes, take several deep breaths, and let each one out with a long sigh. Now, consciously turn your mind to positive thoughts. Focus on someone you love, some activity you enjoy, or a place you would like to be. Keep your eyes closed, continue to breathe deeply and slowly, and keep the image in your mind. This will enable you to reduce the impact of a stressful situation, and you will be giving yourself an instant energy boost.

Behavioral kinesiology also graphically demonstrates how you are affected by other people and their moods. I'm sure you have experienced walking into a room full of people, or meeting a particular person, and immediately feeling discomfort or unpleasantness. The truth of the matter is that your feeling was accurate. We all affect each other nonverbally, just by our presence. Judge this yourself as you conduct this test on your partner.

Instructions:

1. Your partner faces you with one arm at the side of the body and the other arm at a 90° angle to the floor, thumb pointing downward, as in the previous test.

2. Place one of your hands on your partner's shoulder opposite the extended arm. Place your other hand just above your partner's wrist on the extended arm. *(See Figure 1.)* Ask your partner to resist as you push down on the extended arm to establish the level of normal resistance.

3. Instruct your partner to look directly at you. Now begin to frown as you instruct your partner to resist. This time as you push on the arm, continuing to frown, it will usually give way and lower easily.

4. Return to the starting position. This time, smile. Continue smiling while you push on the arm and your partner resists. You will usually discover that the arm will not go down.

When you have completed this exercise, reverse roles and have your partner test you. This exercise can also be conducted with a third person frowning and smiling at your partner while you are testing the arm-resistance.

The Closed Energy Circuit

Were you surprised by the results? This test demonstrates the instantaneous, direct way in which other people can affect your energy level, even by small gestures. A person who frowns visibly, or even within, has an impact on you, although you are generally not consciously aware that it is happening. Conversely, when you frown, you have a negative effect on others. This results in a snowball effect: when one person is in a bad mood, others in the vicinity may become uncomfortable, distressed, or uneasy.

You are not, however, helpless to resist another person's negative energy. The next test will clearly demonstrate that. Repeat the frown and smile test again with one important difference: *Your partner's tongue is to be placed touching the roof of the mouth, approximately one-quarter inch behind the front teeth.* The tongue should be held in this position throughout the frowning and smiling test.

•

What was the result this time? Most likely your partner's arm did not go down when you frowned. Putting the tongue to the roof of the mouth created a closed energy circuit within your partner's body. This made it possible to easily resist the external influence of the frown.

An analogy can be made to walking into a darkened room and turning on a light. When the switch is flipped, the current flows and the energy lights the room. The positioning of the tongue is like an energy button which allows our internal energy to flow, lighting our internal environment. This is one of many behavioral kinesiologic techniques developed by Dr. Diamond. Try applying this energy button to ward off the stresses of the workday. Develop the habit of keeping your tongue in contact with the roof of your mouth.

Lower Back Strain

One tremendous stress for the office worker is stiffness, weariness, and pain in the lower back. While backache is almost universally considered the price of desk work, most non-desk occupations also cause back difficulties. This problem is so pervasive that approximately 80% of all American adults will at some time seek medical attention for back pain.

Estimates are that at least 7 million people receive medical treatment of some type for this misery every single day, and that one out of every three adults is plagued by back pain daily. The insurance industry reports that at least 200 million work days are lost annually due to lower back pain. Chronic back trouble is the single largest drain on industrial compensation funds, costing as much as $10 billion per year.

In the February 1977 issue of *Prevention* magazine, Henry L. Feffer, M.D., professor of orthopedic surgery at George Washington University Medical Center pointed out that the act of sitting, no matter how it is done, puts a lot of stress on the back. "Even when one sits correctly," he said, "the pressure within the spinal discs is still twice that when standing. And the pressure when standing is twice that when lying down."

In addition, a typical working day brings dozens of incidents or pieces of information that arouse strong, active emotions—urgency, impatience, excitement, anger, irritation, and frustration. Our bodies experience the same immediate, intense physical reactions that enabled primitive humans to survive. Adrenalin pours through the system, the heart beats faster, and muscles clench.

Rather than releasing this tension through action—by running, fighting, or hunting—modern civilization demands that we smile graciously at a demanding supervisor or hide our impatience toward a slow trainee, expressing emotions that are different from what we feel.

According to Leon Root, M.D., orthopedic surgeon, in his book *Oh, My Aching Back*, "Emotional stress or tension is just as tiring as physical stress or tension. Emotional fatigue . . . causes your muscles to grow tense and contract. Since your back muscles are constantly working while you are sitting or standing, they are likely to bear the brunt of your emotional fatigue sooner than others."

The more tension your muscles are holding, the more additional tension is created by ordinary movements. Thus, tension increases the risk of injury from normal activities, while causing the person to avoid the stretching and exercise that could relax and heal the muscles.

Finally, a knot of tension or weariness in one muscle puts excess strain on surrounding muscles; they have to do the work of the affected part. Simply supporting a motionless back and spine is work for back muscles. Back pain that starts as a mild annoyance in one spot quickly spreads to other areas, wearing out one's back and sapping one's energy.

Shiatsu for Back Pain

One of the quickest, easiest helps for the back is a two-minute standing or sitting massage which you can do on yourself or on another person. *Shiatsu* means *finger pressure* in Japanese. Without changing your clothes or even wrinkling them, you can treat your back to muscle relaxation and increased circulation and give yourself a general feeling of refreshment and well-being.

This shiatsu treatment consists of applying pressure on prescribed points on the back using both thumbs and pressing each point as hard as you can for five to seven seconds. (Correct shiatsu pressure is described as a cross between pleasure and pain.)

One treatment either gets rid of back pain or greatly speeds the healing process. If discomfort is not gone after the first treatment, simply wait one or two hours and repeat. Continue regular treatments until recovery is complete. I have worked on people for whom one treatment was sufficient, and on others for whom several treatments were necessary.

If pressure on any point is uncomfortably painful, lighten up on that point—some spots may be more sensitive than others. When doing shiatsu on someone else, be sure to tell the person to say ouch if your pressure is painful at any point. Release that point immediately; then go on to the next point and press with normal, hard pressure.

On oneself, three or four times through the points constitutes one treatment; on another person, two or three times is sufficient.

Instructions:

(Adapted from *How to Relax and Enjoy . . .* by Jerry Teplitz with Shelly Kellman, Japan Publications.)

1. Stand, sit, or lie down on a firm surface, whichever position is most convenient and comfortable. (When working on another person, it's easiest to have the person lie down.) Give yourself enough room so that you can easily touch your thumbs to your back. Relax.

2. Begin at the fifth lumbar vertebra. To find it, pretend that your back is divided in halves, top and bottom. From the dividing line, drop down two inches. Press along both sides of the spine (but never directly on the spine) simultaneously, using your thumbs. *(See Figure 2.)*

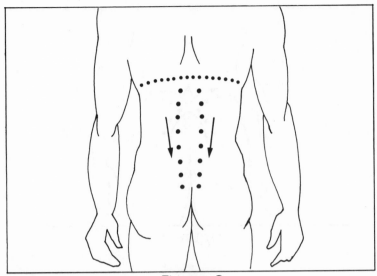

Figure 2

3. Move down along the spine, pressing points at intervals of an inch, until you've pressed beside the tailbone.

4. Find the place where spine and hipbone meet. The hipbone extends across your back above the buttocks. Pressing on both sides simultaneously, follow the hipbone outwards with four pairs of equally spaced points. *(See Figure 3.)*

5. Return to the place where spine and hipbone meet. The next four pairs of points form an inverted *V* to the middle of each buttock.

6. Move to the upper, outer corners of the buttocks and press both sides simultaneously. Repeat at the lower, outer corners. *(See Figure 4.)*

7. Repeat all steps at least once more. If there is still pain or stiffness, do it again. Wait an hour, and repeat full treatment if necessary.

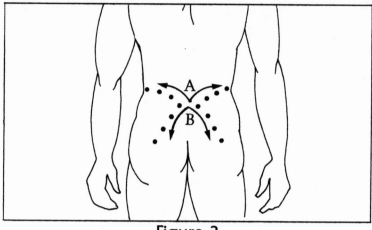

Figure 3

•

Shiatsu reflects the instinctive tendency to rub or press on a sore or aching body part. Various forms of pressure-point treatment have been practiced in the Orient for thousands of years. Shiatsu as we know it was systematized by Tokujiro Namikoshi, founder of the Nippon Shiatsu School, Tokyo.

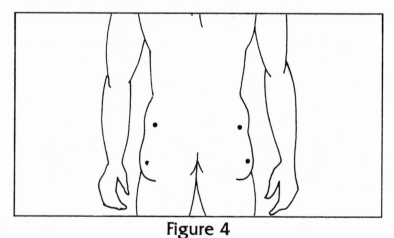

Figure 4

We find that direct pressure relaxes muscles according to the physics principle that every action causes an opposite and equal reaction. Muscles which are pressed and then released respond by stretching and unwinding.

Shiatsu improves blood circulation and muscle metabolism. Combustion of oxygen and glycogen (food energy) within the muscles is necessary for their movement. Both elements are brought in by the blood, through the capillaries, directly to millions of tiny muscle fibers. Circulation brings fresh nutrients to the muscles and prevents a build-up of the waste material lactic acid, which is the actual cause of muscle fatigue.

Circulation is poor in an over-tensed and tired muscle because capillary action is inhibited and metabolism is slowed. Shiatsu stimulates blood vessels to expand, restoring circulation and speeding both the fuel supply and clean-up processes in muscles. That's why treatments are frequently described as "refreshing" or "energizing" as well as relaxing.

Frequent breaks are also of great benefit during long stretches of sitting. The simple act of standing up and walking around one's office, or up and down the hallway, for two or three minutes every hour is more beneficial than half an hour of walking at the end of the day. Every break in the pattern of continuous sitting is a relief from the built-up back tension. It's therapeutic to pace and stretch while dictating letters, listening to recorded material, or talking on the phone.

Shiatsu for Headaches

This Shiatsu treatment has several uses. It takes about a minute and a half, and in that time it can totally alleviate a headache or even a hangover. This treatment will wake up a person who is exhausted from working, playing, or staying up late at night. It will act as a total body relaxant to relieve tension. This technique can be performed on oneself or on others. It works by opening up the blood vessels, restoring circulation, and soothing tight muscles and pain-carrying nerves. You will no longer need aspirin or headache tablets. This therapy is much safer, more effective, and faster than drugs, and there are no possible side effects.

The following directions are written as if you were working on another person; differences for working on yourself are noted in parentheses. (Remember to press each point very hard and for at least three seconds. Tell the person to say ouch if there is pain.)

Instructions:
(from *How To Relax and Enjoy* . . . by Jerry Teplitz with Shelly Kellman, Japan Publications):

1. The person you are working on should be seated upright, glasses off, eyes closed, and in a comfortable position.

2. Standing on the left side of the person, support the forehead with your left hand. (No support is needed when working on yourself.) With the fleshy part of your right thumb—the ball of the thumb—press at the hairline, in the center of the forehead. Move back one inch and press again.

3. Continue pressing points about an inch apart in a straight line from the hairline to the hollow at the base of the skull. *(See Figure 5.)* This hollow is the medulla oblongata. Press it also. (If these points are hard to reach when working on yourself, place your index finger on top of your middle finger. That will give you a similar pressure.)

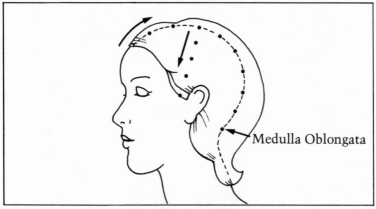

Medulla Oblongata

Figure 5

4. Move slightly to the front of the person. Position your thumbs at the very top of the head. Press with your thumbs, going down the head one inch at a time on both sides simultaneously, to the front middle of the ears.

5. Stand to the person's left again. Now you'll be using your right thumb and middle finger, working at the back of the head. (On yourself, use both thumbs.) Find the middle back of each ear. From there, go straight in one and a half to two inches on each side, toward the medulla. There you'll find a pair of lumps or little nodes. Press simultaneously with thumb and middle finger.

   Move half the distance in towards the medulla on each side. Press both sides. Then place your thumb on the medulla and press. *(See Figure 6.)*

6. Come down the neck one-half inch from the medulla. Place thumb and middle finger on both sides of the spinal column, about an inch apart. (On yourself, use both thumbs.) Don't press on the spinal column; press

right next to it on both sides.

Press three or four pairs of points, depending on how long the neck is. Just go straight down; points are an inch apart. Stop at the shoulders.

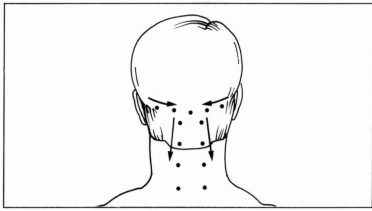

Figure 6

7. Repeat entire process to make one treatment. If the pain has not disappeared, go through the points a third time. (On yourself, you will need to do the treatment three to four times to have total relief.)

•

Stress is all around us. It can pervade everything we do; however, we do not have to be ruled or controlled by it. By practicing some of the techniques in this chapter, you can begin to take charge of your life. You can begin to give yourself the freedom to do what you want to do and feel the way you want to feel. You are responsible for your own health and well-being.

Happy relaxing!

BARBY EIDE

Barby Eide has been a professional speaker and educator for 15 years. She is the first person from Spokane and the first woman in the Northwest's Inland Empire to be nominated and accepted as a member of the National Speakers Association.

Her areas of expertise include time-management, stress- and conflict-management, effective communication, and the psychology of dreams. She also has created two programs especially for today's woman: "Time Management and Organization for Today's Woman," and "Professional Development for Today's Woman." She conducts more than 300 programs a year on these topics for various business, academic, and private organizations.

These educational programs are based on current research studies and developed through practical application in Barby Eide's own life. They offer participants positive ideas and techniques for adding quality and depth to their business, personal, and social experiences.

Letters from clients and students describe Barby Eide as "very professional," "thought-provoking," "progressive," "thoroughly enjoyable," "highly inspiring," and "absolutely smashing."

Her understanding of human behavior, her sensitivity, and her warm humor have made her programs immensely popular. Both she and her work have been featured on many television and radio stations and in numerous publications.

Barby Eide is the author of several published articles and a chapter on stress-management in a medical book, *Go To Health*, published by Nelson-Hall.

In addition to being a successful businesswoman, she serves on the Board of Directors of City College of Spokane and the Spokane Board of Realtors Educational Committee. She is a member of the Spokane Area Chamber of Commerce, the American Society for Training and Development, and several other local and national professional organizations.

Her husband, Leroy M. Eide, is a commercial realtor and financial planning consultant and teaches real estate investment at Spokane area colleges.

The Eides enjoy a variety of outdoor recreational activities together including sailing, skiing, backpacking and traveling.

You may contact Barby Eide by writing to her at Barby Eide & Associates, P.O. Box 2602, Spokane, WA 99220; or telephone (509) 455-8018.

BODY LANGUAGE: WHAT ARE YOU REALLY SAYING?

by BARBY EIDE

You are always telling something about yourself, revealing your innermost feelings. You communicate your true emotions twenty-four hours a day without speaking a single word. Maybe you haven't realized it, but your movements, gestures, facial expressions, and body positions all talk in dozens of little ways. This is often called *body language* or *body talk*. Behavioral scientists have assigned the term *kinesics* to this fairly new area of nonverbal communication.

Amazingly, more than 93 percent of all communication is nonverbal. When you talk with other people, your spoken words make up only 7 percent of the message the listeners receive, formulate, and transcribe in their minds. Without speaking a single word, we tell people who we are, what we are like, and how life is for us at the moment.

Far more revealing than speech, nonverbal communication is an important instrument of self-presentation. Understanding nonverbal communication in ourselves and others can be an important tool for building fulfilling business and social relationships. When you recognize the nonverbal signals and messages you and others are sending, you have learned a language that you can use wherever there are people in your life.

There are many aspects of nonverbal communication that you should be aware of. Some of them are your voice, your posture, the way you dress, your car, and the way you decorate your surroundings.

Your voice. How you speak conveys as much as what you say. Your tone of voice and the speed with which you speak can reflect your emotions, your state of health, your poise, and your confidence. Voices that are clear, well modulated, and vary in pitch, rate, and volume are easy to listen to. Harsh, breathy, and monotonous voices are unpleasant to the ear.

Listen to yourself when you speak. Is your voice rich, full, and vibrant? Does it sound warm, empathetic, and enthusiastic? If you frequently interact with others in your profession, either in person or by telephone, it will be a big advantage to study how you use your voice.

Your posture. The way you sit, walk, and stand can project an image of success and self-confidence; or it can make you look down-and-out, tired, and lethargic. Good posture affects the position of the diaphragm and can make your voice sound pleasant and self-assured. Good posture will also make you look younger and enhance your appearance of health and physical well-being. Your communication with others will benefit.

Your apparel. Everything you wear sends a message. The right clothes can help a person to achieve professional and social success. There are many excellent books on wardrobe. In general, these books tell you to dress appropriately for the situation, choosing clothing that will move you forward rather than hold you back, clothing that will work for you rather than against you.

Not only the cut, style, and fabric of clothing, but also the color communicates something about you and your profession. For instance, it's been found that navy blue and grey tend to inspire trust, while lavender and mustard seem to have the opposite effect. Your business wardrobe can point you toward success, promote your credibility, and strengthen your authority.

As an example, I recently presented a program on stress-management for the president and 18 regional vice presidents of a large bank in the Northwest. We met in the large formal boardroom of the bank's head office and sat around an enormous dark mahogany table. The participants were men, and they all wore dark pin-striped, three-piece suits. I wore a tailored navy blue skirted suit with a crisp white blouse and matching silk scarf.

This particular color combination has been found to create a high authority image for a woman. It tends to give a strong sense of presence, which is especially important for a petite person like me. My executive gold pen and attaché case (an indispensable item for the professional business person) also indicated authority.

What kind of image would I have projected had I worn the dress that is one of my favorites for picnics, drives on summer evenings, and walks with my husband in Spokane's Riverfront Park? If I had worn that dress— flowered, with a bow in the back, pink ribbon around the bodice, and ruffles circling the hem—how would I have been received at the stress-management presentation?

I might not have been able to capture my clients' attention or establish any kind of credibility. I would have been saying that I was dressed for fun and games, not to conduct business. I would not have been accepted as an authority, and the group probably would have had difficulty concentrating on my message.

Appropriately dressed, I communicated without verbalizing that I was there for business, that I knew what I was talking about, that they could trust me, and that I wasn't going to be wasting their business day.

Your car. The vehicle you drive communicates something about you to your clients as well as to the people you meet in traffic. The impression you make will differ according to what kind of car you drive—sports car, pickup truck, expensive luxury car, or small economy car.

Even more important is what your car looks like and how it smells inside. Is it vacuumed? Is it fresh and clean, or is it littered with old newspapers, brochures, hamburger wrappers, and beverage containers? Is the ashtray overflowing, and does the car smell of cigarette or cigar smoke?

Remember that your car is your home or office on wheels. You may have occasion to drive a client who will never call on you at your business address. Your car will speak for you.

Your surroundings. Your furnishings, pictures, and degree of neatness communicate to others. If you work at a desk, what does the top of it say? That you are organized? Or that you are in a muddle and will try to fit your visitor in amid the shuffle somewhere?

Consider the ways we mark our personal territory at the office. Very often we hang a poster or a framed diploma on the wall, or keep personal photos, mementos, or little carved wooden signs on our desks. I recently visited a variety of business offices in the Spokane area with the sole purpose of jotting down some of the sayings I saw on plaques, posters, and signs.

What kind of impression would you get of the individual or business with these signs? On a secretary's desk: "I finally got it all together, but I forgot where I put it."

On a realtor's desk: "Ignorance is an achievement. I'm an over-achiever."

On one receptionist's desk I saw this sign: "Department of sunshine and rainbows. Hopes restored, spirits lifted, enthusiasm renewed."

And on a poster behind another reception desk I found: "I may not be totally perfect, but parts of me are excellent."

This saying was posted on a computer in a public area of a business supply company: "Computer Department—Mistakes While You Wait." (How would you feel about the information you received from that computer?)

A plaque on the desk of a vice president of a supermarket chain said: "Notice—Be Sure Brain Is In Gear Before Engaging Mouth." (One might well feel hesitant about talking freely and openly with this executive!)

First impressions. Your handshake, your hairstyle, and your keychain all reveal something to the people you meet. They create an image that is positive or negative, mature or immature, successful or unsuccessful.

The first impressions others form of you can have a powerful effect on your personal life and your professional career. They can lead people to assumptions about your attitudes, your values, and your abilities. For instance, someone who slouches in a chair, speaks in a dull monotone, lacks good grooming, and is sloppily dressed probably won't inspire as much trust as a clean, neat individual who speaks with sincerity and is assured and well dressed.

If someone could observe you right now, reading this book, what would your posture, your clothing, and your surroundings tell them? Nonverbal communication is especially important during that first 60 seconds after meeting, when people form 70 percent of their opinions.

We know the fallacy of judging a book by its cover, but people still do it, don't they? We make this kind of evaluation all the time. We believe that actions speak louder than words, and often they do. Ralph Waldo Emerson once said: "Do not say things. What you *are* stands over you the while, and thunders so that I cannot hear what you say to the contrary."

The single most important aspect of nonverbal communication is body language. I'd like to share with you a technique to help you use your body language to communicate more effectively with others. The technique is summarized by the acronym SELF IMAGE. Each letter stands for a positive way for you to express yourself through body language. You should practice these steps until this particular technique is second nature.

S—Smile. Keep your smile simple, sincere, and pleasant. If you find your face aching, you're smiling too hard. This commonly occurs at social occasions when we try to appear that we're having a good time, or when we want to please a customer. But it's been found that a too-bright, tense, frozen smile is an annoyance to other people. It may make them feel that you are being plastic or phony.

Smiling is more than a movement of the lips. A genuine smile comes from deep down inside, and the eyes smile at the same time.

E—Eye-Contact. It is important to establish eye-contact with the person you talk to. When someone is shifty-eyed, it gives the impression of being untrustworthy. It makes other people suspect concealment and untruthfulness. But too-intense eye-contact, like a frozen smile, gives negative results. People do not like it when we stare into their eyes directly for a long time. It intimidates them.

Some popular books advocate staring at a person without breaking eye-contact as a means of gaining power. The first person to lower the eyes, in other words, loses. This really seems to me to be a negative approach to communication. It makes an "I win—you lose" situation.

Here is the way to use eye-contact with positive results: When you are talking to others, meet their gaze briefly for a moment, then let your eyes drop and roam over the lower part of their face. Then glance at something you are holding in your hand, such as a drink, or a pen or pencil, before making eye-contact again. Don't be studied about it; if you just let it happen naturally, people should feel very relaxed and comfortable conversing with you.

L—Lean forward. Sit in a manner that indicates interest and enthusiasm, whether you are talking with a customer, your spouse, a child, or a co-worker. Face the person directly, as sitting sideways can say "You're only worth about half of my attention right now." Lean forward a bit, being careful not to invade the other person's space.

Each of us carries around with us special extensions of our personality. We are not limited by the boundaries of our skin. First of all, we have an intimate zone that extends out 6 to 18 inches. This zone is reserved for a very few special people in our lives. We do not like others entering uninvited into this zone, since it is used primarily for intimate contact.

We also have another, slightly larger, personal space bubble that we carry with us wherever we go. This one extends out about 1½ to 2½ feet. We decrease or increase this space depending on how crowded our immediate environment is. We usually feel uncomfortable when another person invades this territory without our permission.

Be aware of how other people react to your closing the distance between you, and watch for nonverbal cues. If a person leans back, becomes rigid, with arms across chest, or begins to blink rapidly, that person may be telling you that you are leaning too far forward.

F—Feet and arms open. Try to keep your posture open. This means having your coat or jacket unbuttoned, your hands open and upturned, if possible, and your legs uncrossed with feet flat on the floor. This posture says that you are confident, relaxed, and not trying to hide anything.

When your coat is buttoned, your arms tightly crossed on your chest, your fists clenched, and your legs crossed, you appear tense and worried. Other people may feel that you are shutting them out.

It's often been said that folded arms mean "I don't buy you or what you're trying to say." They indicate defensiveness and hostility. But the way in which the arms are folded may give other messages, too. Consider that, in general, the higher the arms are folded on the chest, and the more firmly they are crossed, the stronger the gesture of refusal. And if these signs are combined with a frown or a scowl on the face, then the attitude is one of belligerence.

However, if the arms are folded gently and loosely across the lower part of the body, it generally means that the individual is relaxed and in a good mood.

I—Impatience interferes. There are several ways that we can signal our impatience with others. One of these is by jiggling our feet. Some individuals do this with both feet on the floor, thumping their heels or tapping their toes, but it is most common when the legs are crossed.

If you have a lot of nervous energy or are feeling rushed, try to keep both feet flat on the floor. You don't want your feet to tell the other person that you want to get moving, want them to hurry up, don't have time to listen to them. Impatience can also be communicated by drumming fingers on a desk or table top, by clicking a ball-point pen, or by tapping a pencil.

Whether you are talking to a customer or listening to your six-year-old telling about her day at school, keep your feet still and your hands calm and relaxed, and concentrate—really concentrate—on something that interests you about the other person. When you do this your body language will help give the impression you want.

M—Make a few notes. Taking notes can show that you are fully involved in a conversation. There are just a couple of things to remember. First of all, don't take so many notes that the other person feels you are losing the gist of what's being said. Jot down just an item or two as an indication of the importance of the message.

Take care that the words you write down are relevant to the conversation. (Sometimes when someone else is talking our minds wander off and remember all sorts of things we need to do, and we start making note of them. Be sure you don't write *get gas, write Mom, buy milk* while the other person is watching!)

And whatever you do, don't ever let anyone see you doodle! Doodling says to the other person that you have lost interest in the conversation.

A—Attentiveness. When you are listening to someone, nod your head affirmatively. This tells the other person that the message is being received. Tilt your head slightly to show your interest in what's being said. You may want to bring your hand to your face in an evaluation gesture. There are all sorts of ways of doing this; each of us has our own unique way of showing that we are giving careful thought to what's being said.

Be sure that you have a pleasant expression on your face—no scowl or wrinkled forehead. And respond verbally on occasion with noncommittal phrases that will keep the conversation flowing, such as "uh-huh," and "Mmm, that's interesting."

G—Gesture clusters. Body language is made up of gestures, and gestures come in clusters. We can benefit by reading the body language of others, but we may jump to a wrong conclusion if we try to read just one gesture taken out of context. Instead, look at the whole person and at the sum of that person's body language. The more the gestures reinforce one another, the stronger and more certain the message.

Body language varies from culture to culture, and what is acceptable and positive in one country is unacceptable and negative in another. Most of the ideas I've shared in this chapter pertain to our culture in the United States.

E—Express the real you. Be you! It's what's outside that shows, but it's what's inside that counts. Remember always to put first things first. Concentrate on getting to know yourself and on being a real person. A good self-image and a thorough knowledge of your profession, wearing the right clothes, driving the right car, carrying the right size attaché case and an executive gold pen, and using appropriate body language—all these are just frosting on the cake. They will not work for very long or very well if you don't like yourself or the profession you have chosen.

Try to spend time each day to learn who and what you really are, to develop all you want to be and more, from the inside out. Who are you when you're all alone? What are you when you are *you*? Being yourself is what counts most; being real is all that really matters.

Look at your work, your career, your profession. Whether you're the president of a bank, a homemaker, a student, a secretary, a salesperson, or a public speaker—ask yourself: Am I giving the best that is in me to my work? Do I enrich my work by doing it with love? Do I enjoy my work by filling it with joy? Do I enliven and brighten my work with my enthusiasm?

When you have a thorough knowledge of your work and really put yourself into it, you communicate something to others. You can't help but attract opportunities to advance, grow, and share your ideas with others.

Learn to be yourself and love the work that you are doing. Then use your knowledge of body language not only to figure other people out, but also to give others the impressions you want them to have of you.

This excerpt from *Look With the Eyes of Love*, by James Dillet Freeman, expresses my thoughts well:

The world may take me by my title,
or my clothes, or my car,
or my bank balance, or my speech.
But when no one is mouthing my title;
when I have hung up my clothes
and parked my car;
when the bank is shut for the night;
when I am naked in my own room,
in the solitariness of myself . . .

what am I then?
It does not matter much then
whether I am the president
or the general or the holy man.
What matters is that I am myself.
I have to be me.
You have to be you.

VANCE D. NORUM, Ph.D.

Vance Norum, a versatile, creative, and dynamic generalist, has excelled in several diverse disciplines: science and engineering, behavioral science and psychology, education, business, and journalism. He has expertise in the areas of electrical, aerospace and software engineering, counseling and preventive mental health, and Reichian therapy. He has been a university faculty member, a curriculum and seminar design executive, an entrepreneur and founder of several businesses, and has written three books and numerous published articles.

Vance traveled extensively as a child and attended schools in France and Germany. In the late 1940s he was a participant on the distinguished radio program "Quiz Kids."

He holds a B.S. degree in electrical engineering, an M.S. degree in computer science, and a Ph.D. degree in psychology. He is a member of Eta Kappa Nu, Tau Beta Pi, and Sigma Xi honorary fraternities, and is an Associate Fellow of the American Institute of Aeronautics and Astronautics. Vance was the recipient of an Arthur J. Schmitt Foundation scholarship and fellowship for his B.S., M.S., and Ph.D. degree studies.

Vance is also a member of the Psionic Medical Society and the Radionic Association, and is founder of the Integrated Healing Research Foundation, which coordinates the research, clinical, and teaching aspects of preventive holistic medicine. He is now enrolled in medical school and will soon receive his M.D. degree.

You may contact Vance through the Integrated Healing Research Foundation (IHRF), P.O. Box 66457, Los Angeles, CA 90066; or telephone (213) 391-8333.

THE CHALLENGE
OF PERSONAL GROWTH

by VANCE D. NORUM, Ph.D.

Personal growth is a basic process inherent in every human being. Whether or not we choose to acknowledge it, we are constantly growing and changing. We cannot decide not to grow. Just as the cells of our bodies are continuously dying and rejuvenating without our conscious control, aspects of our personalities are also dying and rejuvenating. Old ideas and behaviors give way to new— the feelings of yesterday are not the feelings of today.

Growth and change frighten us. They necessitate giving up what we are familiar with for something as yet unknown to us. For this reason we may refuse to examine the quality of our lives and refuse to take responsibility for the consequences of our emotions and our behavior.

We may close ourselves off to change by sticking rigidly to old habits and old beliefs.

Trauma, such as the death of a friend or the breakup of a relationship, may force us into participating in our own growth. Or sometimes it is a nagging sense that something is missing from our lives that leads us to search for new ways of coping, new ways of experiencing ourselves and our world.

I was originally educated and trained as a scientist in the academic disciplines of engineering, mathematics, and physics. When I became involved in my own personal growth-work, I became profoundly attracted to psychology. My experience has convinced me that our emotional makeup is equally important as the other three facets of personality. Our emotional, spiritual, mental, and physical aspects must all be in balance if we are to lead satisfying lives.

I am going to share with you some of the concepts and experiences I have encountered in my own growth process. I hope that I may encourage you to question, explore, seek, and ultimately respond to this exciting and rewarding challenge.

Growth Issues

Personal growth involves all aspects of our lives. It may be helpful at this point to identify some of the general areas that we may choose to go to work on. Growth issues fall into two basic categories, inner and outer. Inner growth issues involve our general state of being, our self-image, and the way we express feelings and cope with conflict.

Outer growth issues include any area in which we interact with the outer world, such as lifestyle, relationship patterns, and work habits. Outer growth issues are a reflection of the inner condition.

Figures 1 and 2 present questions to serve as a starting point for you in identifying areas of your life which you might like to examine and change.

Beliefs vs. Reality

The goal of all growth-work is to improve how we feel about ourselves. Feelings of inadequacy, lack of self-esteem, and an inability to express emotions in a useful and appropriate way are often the result of erroneous beliefs. A belief is an assumption we make about reality. These beliefs result in the formation of attitudes and their associated behavior programs.

We acquire our beliefs when we are young. From our earliest moments we absorb basic attitudes about ourselves, our emotions, and the world around us. These are the core set of beliefs and values acquired in the first six or seven years of life. When our parents respond negatively to us (or to our behavior), we acquire a corresponding negative belief about who we are. And we mistake the assumption for reality.

If our parents viewed life as a continual struggle, we will have absorbed that belief as a fact: Life is a continual struggle. We then learn to see only the difficult parts of life, as our belief determines which elements of our experience we tune into.

If our parents believed "the world is your oyster" and communicated that to us, today we tend to experience the world as a positive challenge. That is our reality. (When we *expect* to enjoy life, we do enjoy life.) In this way we each create our own reality from our beliefs and attitudes.

Similarly, if our parents did not allow open expressions of anger, they communicated to us that anger was

---

Figure 1
Inner Growth Issues

How do I feel about myself from day to day?

Do I like myself?
Do I feel adequate in relation to others?
Do I enjoy being alone with myself?
Do I often criticize myself?

How do I express my feelings and emotions?

Am I honest and direct in letting others
know how I feel?
Do I have periodic unexplainable outbursts
of emotion?
Do my moods fluctuate often and
uncontrollably?

How do I approach conflict and stress?

Do I feel positive and confident in my
ability to cope?
Do I tend to blame others for my failures?
Am I often overwhelmed by day-to-day
conflicts?
Do I see challenges as burdens or as
challenges?

How do I make decisions?

Do I rely on other people's opinions?
Do I look to others to validate my decisions?
Do I value others' advice about my own
feelings?
Do I need approval to feel good about myself?

Figure 2
Outer Growth Issues

How do I feel about my work situation?

Do I find my work challenging and
creative, or boring and unstimulating?
Am I able to assert myself with my boss and
my colleagues?
How do I cope with job-related stress?

Are my relationships generally positive or negative?

Are my relationships predictable?
Do I project my emotional needs onto others?
Are my expectations unrealistic?
Do I make unreasonable demands?
Do I get locked into roles?
Am I secure in my personal identity,
or do I tend to define myself in terms
of my relationships?
Do I feel less of a person when I am not
involved with someone?

*Have I translated my inner values into a satisfying
lifestyle?*

Do I choose friends who share and
support my values?
Do I arrange my work schedule to fit my
inner needs?
Do my activities enhance my well-being?
Do I value social convention over my
own feelings?

wrong. As adults we are then apt to find that even minor conflicts are highly stressful. We habitually repress our anger and expect others to do the same.

The constant repression of feeling causes an emotional imbalance. Feeling becomes intensified and distorted by repression. Sooner or later it will surface in an inappropriate way. This is why a person who represses anger may experience sudden unexplainable outbursts of temper.

This cycle of repression, distortion, and eruption of emotions plays a very important part in personal growth issues.

Let's use a hypothetical example to show how our beliefs determine our emotions and behavior. Mr. X suffers from frequent bouts of depression. He thinks that his emotions just come over him "from out of the blue."

Now if Mr. X were to examine his thought patterns carefully, he would discover negative beliefs about himself. They are invisible to him, for they operate below his level of awareness. He sees them not as beliefs, but as indisputable fact.

Some of these assumptions might be, "I'm no good—nothing I do will be good enough," "I'm weak and helpless," "I'll always be a failure—it's hopeless to try," or "I don't deserve to succeed."

When Mr. X learns to stop at the moment he begins to feel depressed and ask himself "What was I just thinking that triggered this feeling?" he will begin to regain a sense of control over his life.

We must recognize our own intimate responsibility for our personal state of being. We *choose* which beliefs to accept, and we *create* for ourselves life experiences that reflect them. We must spot the belief and change it before the feelings will change.

The Growth Process

There are many ways in which you can facilitate your own growth. Each conflict situation can be a source of growth and change for you, if you recognize that in each of your responses you are making a choice. You are moving toward growth, or against it, moving with it or away from it.

In addition to your awareness of participation in your own personal growth, there is a seven-step process of holistic integration that can serve as a useful guide to your explorations. It consists of *commitment, identifying issues, risk-taking, working with feelings, correlation and evaluation, reprogramming,* and *growth maintenance.*

Commitment. The decision to consciously explore our basic assumptions and to take action to change them is the first step toward wholeness. We might not arrive at commitment in one flash of insight. It is often a more gradual process: we find ourselves drawn to people, ideas, and experiences that embody the creative growth principles; growth issues take on a new priority; we begin to challenge lifelong values and roles; and we experience an openness to new ways of looking at ourselves that creates the potential for new and original experiences.

We might take a new interest in dreams, remembering them more frequently and with increasing vividness. In a sense, our unconscious responds to our new willingness to explore by making inner material available to us.

We may become more receptive to our reactions in daily life situations. Because of our conscious decision to participate in our growth, we may begin to see many aspects of our life in a different light.

A high-priority commitment is essential to continued progress in growth work. It keeps us involved when the going gets tough.

Identifying issues. After commitment, the next step in facilitating the growth process is identifying issues.

To identify the issues that will figure in your own growth process, examine your attitudes, beliefs, and feelings. Look at your relationships, your job, and your lifestyle. This will give you an initial direction. Make two separate lists, identifying inner growth issues and outer growth issues. (Consult Figures 1 and 2 for a beginning.)

Try to get clear on what you want to change about the way you feel and act. The inner issues are the foundation from which we enter life situations. Obviously we cannot have healthy relationships or confidence in our work if our self-image is poor.

Risk-taking. The next basic process of holistic integration involves attitude. After making growth issues a high priority and identifying specific problems, we must consciously work on our attitude toward our discoveries. We must desire to perceive ourselves objectively, to risk letting go of our defenses. Instead of accepting our defensive behavior, we must challenge those defenses and try to see what need they are serving. What are they protecting us from?

We risk the possibility that our current self-image is biased, inaccurate, and a lot less ideal than we have believed. We face the negative consequences that our defenses and manipulations have had on others. We confront our illusions. We risk the pain of realities that we have previously chosen not to see.

But as we confront these negative areas in our personalities, we must also recognize that our defenses, projections, and illusions have all served some positive purposes. These defense mechanisms developed to protect the ego and preserve our basic integrity. We need them until we are strong enough and integrated enough to face the pain that triggered them in the first place.

So in a sense, this third step involves two simultaneous attitudes: One of challenging, confronting, and risk-taking; the other of trusting and believing in ourselves.

This process can result in an awareness of when it is appropriate and positive to surrender our defenses and an ability to do this when we choose to.

Working with feelings. All the insight in the world by itself cannot eliminate negative emotions. It must be accompanied by a full experience of the emotions themselves. Like the return of the prodigal son and the lost sheep, our repressions *contain legitimate aspects of ourselves* which must be recovered if we are to be whole.

Each emotion has an appropriate and rightful place in our daily experience. Anger, fear, grief, and hatred are all part of the human condition and have inherently positive purposes. It is our negative beliefs about our emotions that cause us to fear them.

We are usually very threatened by an emotion we have repressed. The emotion has become intensified and distorted over the years: by denying it and viewing it as undesirable, we have made it into a monster. It becomes an "emotional Adam," which can burst under any stimulus and unleash inappropriate emotional energy to cause pain and turbulence in our daily lives.

Working with feelings on a deep level is a crucial part of personal growth. While there is no set path to follow, this basic, six-step process provides some useful guidelines.

1. Acknowledge your feelings. Let down your defenses enough to admit painful emotions. This is essentially a step in being honest with yourself.

2. Give yourself permission to let go. Take full responsibility for allowing feeling. A safe and supportive environment is important here.

3. Focus attention on what is happening within you. Keep your energy on your feelings even though they may be painful or threatening. Think as little as possible. It is easy to rationalize and use thinking as a defense.

4. Get involved with your feelings. As they begin to surface, actively and consciously participate in them. Choose to be involved with a given feeling and allow it to intensify.

5. Surrender to your feelings and totally accept them. Give up all control and experience feelings without judgment at their fullest intensity. This step can be scary at times and often requires you to be in the presence of at least one person who can accept you being out of control.

6. Discharge the blocked energy contained in repressed feelings. Use movement and vocalization to act out feelings and release them. This is the step of catharsis.

When you are willing to experience your emotions, you will find that your repressed pain, fear, guilt, and grief will begin to surface. Do not, however, expect all your repressions to be externalized in one session. This is a continuing process. Throughout your life you will use emotional externalization techniques—after all, expressing your emotions is an integral part of living!

Correlation and Evaluation. Although externalizing the emotions is a positive step forward, it will not, in itself, effect permanent change. The discharged emotions will accumulate anew unless you also correlate them with the underlying attitudes and the behavior associated with them.

In a sense, these two processes are two sides of the same coin. On one side is emotion and on the other is cognition. Both are needed to effect lasting change.

Do I believe I am unworthy of love? Do I believe I am incapable of success? Do I believe I am unattractive and undesirable? Once you have identified the assumption which is responsible for a particular problem, you then evaluate your belief in terms of its truth and value. Does this assumption deny or limit my potential? Does this belief make me feel good about myself? How does this belief motivate me to act toward other people—positively or negatively? This process is also one of seeing clearly how you create your own reality and accepting total responsibility for it.

Reprogramming. Finally, you create new beliefs to replace the discarded ones. These new, positive beliefs might be: I am lovable; I deserve success; I can earn all the money I need; I can achieve whatever I want to achieve; I am strong and effective.

Actually feeling these new beliefs, however, takes time and effort. A good exercise is to begin making lists of your positive and negative beliefs. Write as quickly as possible to minimize censoring from your "inner judge." Sometimes we are so accustomed to our negative beliefs that we can barely manage to think of positive ones. It may even be difficult to make the pen write the words!

Realize that you are literally building new neuronal pathways. You are not used to these new beliefs, just as you once were not used to solving math problems, or reading French. Bring the negatives out into the open. See them for what they are. Reinforce and recreate the beliefs you want to hold.

As integrated adults, we finally reach the stage where we consciously choose the beliefs that direct our lives. We gain control over our emotions and behavior through expanded self-awareness. We can now use our energies creatively to further explore our deeper potentials. This occurs after we have exposed the negative assumptions that have controlled our behavior, corrected them, and revised our emotional responses. We have created positive new beliefs and appropriate responses in their stead. Our behavior is now reprogrammed to be self-directed and self-actualized.

Growth Maintenance. Growth maintenance is a state of mind. After we have reprogrammed ourselves, we keep ourselves open to the new and creative elements within us. We remain sensitive to any blocks or impediments that build up. We view our personal growth as a way of life, utilizing growth processes as needed to continually clear ourselves of negative beliefs and the distorted emotions they cause. We open inner doors to original psychological experiences and new life patterns, and achieve an ever-increasing sense of well-being.

Focusing

While specific processes for integration are helpful tools of growth, the most valuable tool of all cannot be taught. This tool is the ability to focus inward—to listen to the subtle feelings and sensations within us that we are usually too busy or too defensive to heed. These feelings contain our deep and personal truth.

While no one can be taught the experience of inner focusing, guidelines can help a person to experience it for oneself.

Create an environment of solitude. Set aside a certain period each day to spend with yourself. Let it be in a special place in your home, a quiet corner of your bedroom, by a window with your favorite trees—whatever place enhances your feeling of being with your self.

Relax. Sit or lie in a comfortable position. Focus your attention on your breathing. Feel your breath moving in and out and visualize your breath cleansing your body of tension and anxiety. Relax your entire body.

Focus on a problem. Suppose you have noticed that you feel uncomfortable around a friend. Focus on these feelings. Sometimes they will express themselves through imagery, a kind of dream in a waking state. Give the imagery plenty of time to unfold. See what it tells you.

(In this case, perhaps you may realize that your friend reminds you of your older sister. Tune into your feelings about your sister. Perhaps there was unacknowledged competition between you, which made you feel inferior. Maybe the similarity of your friend's personality is acting as a hook for those buried feelings.)

Act out your feelings. In addition to imagery, you may experience bodily sensations. You may find your body stiffening all over, or slumping downward. You may desire to stomp around the room or sit in a heap on the floor. Let your body tell you how to move.

Verbalize. If you feel a strong desire to verbalize with the movement, do so. But keep the words to a minimum. Try to find just one sentence that fits your feeling. Focus closely on each word you try out, and keep experimenting until you find the combination that gives you a sense of having clearly and fully expressed yourself.

When you achieve insight about the basis of your problem, a whole area of your emotional life will begin to return to you. You will be able to work with your feelings, now that they are out in the open. You will recover an exiled but valuable portion of yourself.

The Structure of Personality

Understanding the structure of personality can be very helpful to us when we pursue a program of personal growth. Of the many theories of personality, two current theories adequately reflect the holistic nature of man's being: C. G. Jung's Theory of Types, and L. A. Hinshaw's Four-Quadrant Model of Personality.

Both deal with the interaction of the four major facets of the personality: intellectual, spiritual, emotional, and physical. Both are based on the assumption that the four dimensions or quadrants are dynamically interconnected. Damage (such as rejection, loss of love, or illness) in any one quadrant will affect the remaining three. Physical illness, for instance, affects our emotions, our intellect, and our spiritual perspective. Similarly, a positive spiritual outlook can affect our bodies, our minds, and our emotions. Such an outlook can turn a trauma into a positive and growthful challenge.

Jung's theory grew out of his vast clinical experience in which he observed that people use their minds in many different ways. He reasoned that the building blocks of these differences were four processes common to all our functioning: sensation, intuition, thinking, and feeling. We get information about our world through sensation (the five senses) or intuition (a hunch, a sudden inspiration or insight); we make judgments or evaluations about our world based on thinking (logical analysis) or feeling (like or dislike). The ways in which each of us prefer to use these processes or functions create our individual differences. This is why two people can have very different reports of the same experience.

It is extremely helpful to learn which functions are well developed in us and which are not, and whether we direct these functions outwardly, to people, things, and institutions (extroverted), or inwardly to concepts, ideas, and values (introverted). If we realize that each of us views things through different channels—and that each channel is equally valid—we can open up possibilities for communication where none previously existed.

L. A. Hinshaw expanded Jung's theory into the Four-Quadrant Model of Personality. His work is a synthesis of Jung's concepts and additional theories developed by Helen Craw of the Helen Craw Theosophical Foundation in San Diego, California.

The Craw-Hinshaw model hypothesizes that the four interlocking quadrants—intellectual, spiritual, emotional, and physical—each contain an instinctive drive for development. We have instinctive drives for survival, for procreation, for physical growth, and for spiritual growth (self-actualization). These drives are equal in energy, although they do not emerge simultaneously.

The emergence of the drive for spiritual growth, for instance, depends upon fulfillment of our needs for physical survival. But the spiritual drive is no less important or necessary than our survival instincts.

The energy in each quadrant is distributed through eight universal attributes which characterize and differentiate the flow of energy throughout the personality. The attributes comprise four sets of opposites: independence-dependence, introversion-extroversion, aggression-submission, and nonconformance-conformance. Ideally, there is a natural and balanced flow between these opposites, often referred to as rhythmic balance.

Each attribute emerges during an appropriate state of our total development from infancy to mature adulthood.

When these attributes are not distorted by negative beliefs, our personalities develop along positive lines. If negative beliefs are pervasive, however, these attributes become correspondingly distorted. Figure 3 shows the relationship between the quadrants, the attributes, and their distorted and nondistorted expression. The rhythmic balanced state exists when there is no distorted expression in any attribute of the quadrants.

Using the Four-Quadrant model as a springboard, some investigative questions you might put to yourself are:

- Is my aggression exaggerated to the point of intrusion, domination, tyranny, or control over others?

- Is my nonconformance exaggerated and distorted to the point of rebelliousness?

- Is my submission exaggerated and distorted so that I play the role of the martyr, the victim, or the masochist?

- Is my extroversion exaggerated and distorted to the point of being obnoxious or exhibitionistic?

- Is my dependence exaggerated and distorted so that I cling to relationships in an unhealthy way?

- Is my conformance exaggerated or distorted so that I am rigid and inflexible in my ideas and judgments?

- Is my introversion exaggerated and distorted so that I passively withdraw from relationships and responsibilities?

- Is my independence exaggerated and distorted so that I put myself above needing other people and act with arrogance and superiority?

Figure 3

PERSONALITY QUADRANT	ATTRIBUTE	DISTORTED BEHAVIORAL QUALITY	NONDISTORTED BEHAVIORAL QUALITY
Intellectual	Aggression	Domination, power trip	Assertion, self-expression, creativity
Intellectual	Nonconformance	Rebellion	Originality, individuality
Physical	Submission	Passivity, bitterness	Good judgment, prudence, dynamic patience
Physical	Extraversion	Clowning, hyperactivity	Friendly, outgoing, at ease with the outer world
Emotional	Dependence	Clinging, clutching	Cooperation, mutual support
Emotional	Independence	Rigidity, narrow-mindedness	Moderation, respect for tradition
Spiritual	Independence	Indifference	Self-reliance
Spiritual	Introversion	Resignation, withdrawal	Introspection, self-knowledge

Selecting a Growth Process

Selecting a therapy or growth process that's right for you involves, above all, an examination of your own needs and personal goals. The selection process itself is an integral part of growth-work. Investigate the available methods, therapies, groups, processes, and therapists and observe your responses closely. Try to clarify why some approaches appeal to you and others do not. Be careful to examine your reasons for rejecting a process—you may be projecting your own negative beliefs and feelings. This may lead you to avoid a potentially fruitful program.

Probably the most important factor in growth-work is the degree of commitment you feel. Ask yourself, "Do I have a desire to give up my negative thought patterns and behaviors? Do I have the time and energy to do justice to this endeavor? Am I able to suspend some of my current attitudes and beliefs in order to explore the principles of this new approach to life? Am I willing to give growth-work the highest priority?"

Free choice is a crucial element in your decision to seek therapy. While most people are not openly coerced into growth or therapy, subtler forms of pressure and manipulation can diminish your freedom of choice. You must honestly consider whether you are doing this to help yourself or to please someone else. Are you doing it out of fear or guilt, or because you feel a deep desire within you to begin this type of journey?

Once you are clear on where you are coming from, you can evaluate the growth processes themselves. You can make *pragmatic* evaluations: (Do these growth processes work consistently—do they deliver what was promised or advertised?); *intellectual* evaluations: (Are these growth processes reasonable?); *emotional* evaluations: (How do I feel about experiencing these processes?); and *spiritual* evaluations: (Are these growth processes consonant with my world view?).

Finally, notice how you feel about the leaders of any program you choose. Do the leaders practice what they preach? *It is absolutely essential that the leaders have personally experienced the processes they seek to facilitate in others.* Are they good examples for you? Can you sense the benefits of the growth process through them? Do you feel comfortable and at ease around them? Do you feel that they respect where you are coming from?

If you have any doubts about the program leaders or suspect the sincerity of their motives, follow your intuition and look elsewhere for guidance. The ultimate criterion for selecting any growth process is *how you feel about it.*

•

The challenge of personal growth is ultimately a transforming experience. In accepting this challenge, we seek not only to heal our wounds, but to explore the further reaches of our being. We are no longer satisfied with the old medical model of sickness and health, normal and abnormal. Through the Human Potential Movement, a new vision of man has been crystallized—a vision where the static and limited emotions of "normal" are replaced by the search for new regions of consciousness.

The inherent wholeness of man's being replaces the dichotomy of mind and body that has divided us for so long. The goals of holistic integration, psychosynthesis, and self-actualization inspire us to new heights of creative fulfillment.

The climate of our times is undeniably one of searching, transformation, and growth. Each of us is part of this climate. Each of us contributes to a greater evolution when we personally explore our own inner dimensions.

By accepting the challenge of our own personal growth, by accepting the inner journey of consciousness, we make our most valuable contribution—that of personal truth, the gift of individual integrity.

J. BARRY PATCHETT

J. Barry Patchett began his public career in 1958. After beginning studies to be a funeral director, Barry found his way into the broadcasting industry, first as a disc jockey, then later as Professor Tassel, a children's television performer. Later he became assistant manager of the television station, continuing his 'on-air' status and assuming responsibility for all studio and commercial production.

In 1972 Barry started a second career—this one in real estate. In just six short months he was a million-dollar sales agent. With his usual drive to meet new challenges head on, Barry became a project sales manager for a high-rise condominium offering more than 800 units for sale. The building was sold out in two years.

In 1977 Barry joined a national real estate franchise organization as an instructor. In seven months he was appointed director of training for the Middle Atlantic region. Barry gained area prominence by teaching real estate courses. He developed a financing marketing program, "Creative Financing: an alternate plan" which he has presented throughout the country.

1979 was a big year for Barry. He was accepted as a member of two professional speakers groups, The National Speakers Association and the International Platform Association.

Barry manages his speaking and training schedules through his own corporation, Personal Dimensions, Inc. He is also vice president and sales manager of Heritage Realty Company, Inc., a company that grew from nothing to ten residential sales offices and more than 200 sales associates in less than a year.

When time permits, Barry relaxes with his wife, Joan, at their waterfront home near Chesapeake Bay in Maryland.

You may contact Barry Patchett by writing to him at 325 Sturtons Lane, Pasadena, MD 21122; or by telephoning (301) 437-1310.

TO CATCH A DREAM

by J. BARRY PATCHETT

Have you ever said to yourself "Someday I'd like to . . ." or "Someday I'd like to be . . ."? Well, that's a dream. It's *your* dream. And your dream can become reality.

In his book *Certainly Dreams Come True*, Dr. Norman Vincent Peale writes that at the end of our days, when we come before the Heavenly Throne, we will be asked to account for our dreams: "I gave you some bright and wonderful dreams when you were young. What did you do with them? Did you let them lose their luster? Did you let them grow tawdry? Or did you keep those dreams bright and shining all the way?"

As a boy back in Talbot County, on Maryland's eastern shore, I remember being the neighborhood promoter.

Puppet shows, backyard carnivals—you name it, I promoted it. I was dreaming then of being a professional promoter.

Being a promoter was not a common desire for a youngster; most of my friends wanted to be firemen, doctors or lawyers. My Mom and Dad weren't quite sure about my ambition, but they encouraged my dream. Nevertheless it didn't quite work out the way I planned. Although I've been active in community theater groups and civic and fraternal organizations, I've never promoted a carnival or puppet show professionally. The dream changed along the way.

The song of Broadway play and movie fame, "There's No Business Like Show Business," tells about becoming a star overnight: ". . . the next day on your dressing room they hang a star." However, most dreams do not come true overnight. "Overnight" for many of us amounts to years of dedication and determination, but in the Bible we are told that our tithes will be rewarded tenfold. Imagine what it will mean to have your dream rewarded tenfold!

•

What was your childhood dream? Do you still see it in your mind's eye, or has it faded? Most people lose sight of their dreams in the course of their lives. As they get married, have children, and relocate to other parts of the country, their dreams change. Have circumstances changed your dream? No matter. You still have that dream, and it's the important part of your life.

Not long ago a great dream came true for me when the day-to-day operations of a large corporation were placed in my hands. Then suddenly that dream came crashing down. Because of upper-level management changes, I was given the choice of moving to a distant location or leaving the corporation. Needless to say, I wanted to leave, and fast. I was crushed to the point of total defeat. But my wife helped me to rebuild my dream. I transferred to the smaller-scale operation and I worked hard. Slowly I began to develop new dreams to replace the old. It was as if I were starting over in my life.

As you read this, how do you picture your dream in your mind's eye? That dream that you see has the power to change your life and the life of your family and friends.

Many people have said in many ways, "What the mind can conceive and believe, it can achieve." You have conceived an idea—a dream. Do you believe in it? Believing in your dream is the same as believing in yourself. You must believe in yourself to make your dreams come true.

•

A dream is like taking a trip. You want to go from where you are now to where you want to be. When you go to the supermarket, you really don't need to plan your trip. You can almost get there with your eyes closed. But heading into unfamiliar territory requires some planning and a good road map. A map will help you to avoid wrong turns. Without it you run the risk of getting off the track, getting lost, losing your dream.

Dr. Martin Luther King said: "I had a dream. I've been to the mountain."

Here is a map to take you to *your* mountain. There are three basic steps to following your dream. They are: 1. Write it down. 2. Reinforce it. 3. Involve the family.

Write down your dream. Dreams are wonderful, but they are also elusive and must be captured on paper. Put your dream down on paper just as you see it. (There was only one Hemingway—so don't worry about how you write—just write!)

Let me make a suggestion: Keep a pad and pencil handy on your night stand. The kind of dreams we are discussing often come during sleeping hours, and they are so vivid that they really seem to be happening. You need to write these down as soon as you wake.

One of my first jobs was as an insurance investigator. It didn't take me long to become dissatisfied. That job seemed a little dull—well, more than a little dull! What I really wanted to be was a disc jockey. At the time, of course, I had no experience or training in the field, but I wrote that dream down exactly as I wanted it to happen.

For some time, personal circumstances prevented me from working on that dream. Then one day it occurred to me to find someone in the broadcasting field who would critique tape recordings of my efforts. I purchased the most inexpensive tape recorder that Sears sold, a bulky reel-to-reel model. It had a microphone with a cord about four feet long. Every night for weeks I sat reading the newspaper into that tape recorder. My Mom and Dad just looked at me. I'm sure they thought that I was wasting my time.

As soon as I made a recording I thought was good enough, I drove over to the radio station in the next town, about 16 miles away. I waited on the steps of the station for an announcer to come through the door. When one finally did, I said, "Hey, look—I've got a tape here and I'd like you to hear it and tell me how I can make it better." The announcer did not share my enthusiasm. He looked at me as if he wished I would go away. But I didn't go away, and finally he agreed to listen to it.

We put the tape on, and I watched the smile on the announcer's face gradually fade. He shook his head in disbelief at all the mistakes he was hearing. I told him that was exactly why I had brought the tape to him—I knew I needed to improve my delivery. So he gave me some pointers and sent me home with some news copy from the wire-service machine. I was to practice it and come back when I thought I had it right.

A week later I was back. We went through the same procedure for the next four months. You can't believe the time I spent working on those tapes! Record. Erase. Record again. Erase again. Over and over. I spent every spare moment of my time this way. But I was learning.

At the end of those four months my dream came true. I quit my job as an insurance investigator and went to work as a disc jockey. Because I had written my dream down, I never lost sight of it. Every day I saw that dream fulfilled. (If you want your dream to become reality, write it down!)

Reinforce your dream. You need to reinforce your written dream in your mind at least twice every day. Many people I know write their dream on a 3 × 5 card and then place that card where they can easily see it at their place of work. They reaffirm their dream three times a day for the five working days. If you are in a hurry to have your dream fulfilled, you might want to use a "3 × 7" program and reinforce your dream three times a day, *seven* days a week.

It is not impossible or improbable to work on several dreams at once. In fact, concentrating on a single idea may not be the best approach for you.

About a year ago I met Lee Miller, a "man on the move." Lee told me he was working simultaneously on 17 dreams. My immediate response was "How do you keep track of them?" His system sounded amazingly effective. Since he was in sales and spent a lot of time driving, he had turned his car into a "dreamboat" by installing a cassette tape player. He recorded all 17 of his dreams on the tape at about one-minute intervals, with background music in between. (He told me it was necessary to change the tape frequently, because his dreams kept coming true!)

If your drive to work takes just 15 minutes each way, you can use that time to reinforce your dream. That will give you two reinforcements daily. Review it again when you wake and upon retiring. That's a total of four reinforcements each day. Already you are exceeding the basic 3 × 5 system; you can be sure your dream will become reality.

Involve the family! Don't keep your dreams a big secret. There's no point in trying, because whatever your dream, it most assuredly will affect your family. Enlist their help in making it come true. Consider that if your dream is to lose weight and your wife is the national prize winner in the Pillsbury Cake, Pudding, and Pie Contest, without her help you could be in trouble!

My friend Lola's husband, Frank, was a sports buff. Her dream was for Frank to buy a second television set so he could watch sports in the den. Now that wasn't a gigantic dream, but it was impossible to achieve without involving Frank. You see, Frank was the guy who was to pay for the new TV!

Lola had to convince him that a new TV was necessary. (It's one thing for Frank to spend money on a six-pack of beer—but a new television, that's something else!) I helped Lola work out a way to get his support, and in a short time her dream came true and the TV sports scene was moved out of the living room.

Lola sold the "You Benefit." In this case it was that Frank could have sports parties in the den and his friends and he could all enjoy the new super-wide 5-foot screen together.

Remember, whenever others are involved they are

asking themselves "What's in it for me?" When you answer this question for them, you can usually get anything you want. Just ask Lola.

•

Do you ever wonder where some people get their seemingly boundless energy? They can pack as much work into one day as you do in two. You almost need stop-action photography to see them, they move so rapidly. The source of their energy is a great personal excitement that comes from their efforts to catch their dream. That excitement could be called *desire.*

Why do you get out of bed in the morning? Most people would answer "To pay the mortgage" or "To put food on the table," or something similar. Do those answers seem exciting to you? Are they your answers? They shouldn't be. Life is far too short to be that dull.

My Dad worked for the same company, doing the same job, for 18 or 20 years. He had been a farm boy, one of 12 children, and like many rural youngsters at that time had attended a one-room school house through sixth grade. He made good money and provided adequately for his family, and he thought himself one of the luckiest men in town.

Every morning Dad got out of bed excited because he had a job to go to and a loving family to love. To him these meant everything. But he was also a dreamer. He dreamed that his son would accomplish more than he, achieve even greater success. All his dreams were focused on me instead of himself.

The problem with this sort of dream is that the end result of my dad's dream was determined by *my* desire, not his. If he had dreamed of me being President of the United States, I might have been, but only if *I had had the desire.* (Obviously, I lacked that desire!)

Youngsters today seem to have more than their share of problems with drugs and delinquency. Why? Because they have no dreams, no reason to get up in the morning. Some people call them "bad" kids. I don't believe that. Others will say they have "bad" parents. I don't believe that either.

What I do believe is that something is lacking today in the relationship between parents and their children. While every physical need may be provided for, many children grow up without knowing how to love and be loved. Without love people become depressed, anxious. They live without a dream for their lives.

•

Not long ago a 15-year-old runaway girl stayed with my wife and me for about six days. This girl, whom I'll call Leslie, had run away from her home in California, zig-zagging her way across the country by hitchhiking some 3500 miles. She was headed back to Washington, D. C., where she had lived next-door to us before the family moved to California. The police had picked her up for curfew violation in the Virginia suburbs and were holding her in the county detention center for juveniles.

When I asked Leslie why she ran away from home, she thought for a moment and then replied "I'm not sure."

As we talked, we eliminated various reasons usually given by runaways. The bottom line for Leslie was that she did not feel loved. Her mother often worked overtime and didn't have time to talk with her, and she couldn't share her personal feelings with her two brothers.

Leslie ran away because she was trying to catch her dream, to find love. While I do not propose that you use Leslie as a model, she had the right idea. If you expect your dreams to come true you have to act to put some life into them—you have to put excitement into your dream.

Many times people have said to me, "I know how to set goals—how to dream. I do everything you say, but my dreams never come true." In talking with these people I've found that they neglect one thing; they really don't desire their dream. The desire comes from someone else. They are trying to please others, not themselves.

While the feelings of others are important, it's your own feelings, your own desires, that are essential in pursuing a dream. No one can catch that dream of yours for you!

All the reasons that dreams slip away are controlled by you. Remember the three basic steps: *write it down, reinforce it* and *involve the family.* Add to these one secret ingredient: one large helping of desire extracted from within, sprinkled generously and stirred vigorously.

Don't worry about setting a goal you can never reach. You will never seriously desire anything you can't possibly have. If you can get truly excited over something, then it *can and will* be yours. Productive desire is *real.* It will never leave you alone. It will be there in your mind, prodding and poking. It won't let you be satisfied until you achieve your dream.

Several years ago I weighed 195 pounds and it is my dream to weigh 195 pounds again. Every day I create the desire within myself to lose that weight by picturing myself buttoning the coat and vest to one of my favorite suits. Every day I affirm to myself, "I look and feel my best at 195 pounds." I'm a great-looking guy with my coat buttoned!

•

Remember that dreams come in all shapes and sizes. They will change as you change. The dream you bring to reality may be different from the one with which you started, and that's okay if that's what you want. There are dreams that become reality in just a few days or weeks, while others take months or years to accomplish.

Just recently, I was attending a three-day seminar in Philadelphia, the Adventures In Attitudes program, sponsored by Personal Dynamics Institute. On the morning of the third day, we had just concluded a group discussion and Joan, the leader, began to give her report. As she began speaking, her voice gave way. She sat down abruptly, put her face in her hands and began to cry.

It seemed that Joan had been struggling with a marital problem for well over a year and she suddenly realized, right there in Philadelphia, that she had been chasing the wrong dream. Right then and there she wrote down her new dream, which she shared with us. Her dream was to take charge of her life and to make her own decisions.

It seemed that Joan had been living in a world dominated by her husband. Joan had continued her career while being a wife and a mother to two small children. Her husband, though, was complaining more and more about her career.

Joan decided that she would not lose her identity. She was a real person and would remain so, but she would be a better and happier person starting right then.

What was the result for Joan, a happier marriage or a separation? I don't know. I haven't seen her or talked with her since that time, but just as surely as I relate this to you, her life is better and happier as she wished it to be.

•

How about your dreams? Do they unlock the energy within you? Do they create the desire that will make them come true? Energy for your dream cannot be created in you. But it is there—a great and powerful sleeping giant waiting only for the alarm clock to ring. Only you can set the timer on the alarm clock. That's when you have your dream. The mere fact that you hold this book in your hand shows that you have a dream and that you want to catch that dream. It's time—right now—to write it down. It's time—right now—to begin the chase.

Watch out! Even from this distance I can hear you saying, "You bet I'll write it down—just as soon as I get a 3 × 5 card."

Now is the time to write it down! Not tomorrow—right now! So here at the end of this chapter I am giving you space to write. Use it right now! The longer you delay, the longer you'll have to wait for your dream to be caught.

Oral Roberts concludes his broadcasts each week by saying, "Something wonderful is going to happen to you." That's true. Believe in yourself and in your dream and the most wonderful thing will happen—your dream will become reality.

Write Down Your Dream—Right Now!

LUNDA HOYLE GILL

Lunda Hoyle Gill, artist and adventurer, has a special interest in tribal cultures. She is recording these cultures
on canvas from life as an added dimension to their pres-
ervation. Lunda gathers her material on location, painting the people in their native habitats. She has painted
the Eskimos on St. Lawrence Island in the Bering Sea; the
Kikuyu, Masai, and Samburu in Kenya; the Aborigines in
Australia; the Balinese in Indonesia; the Morind in Irian
Jaya; and the tribes in Papua New Guinea. She has
painted many of the Indian tribes of the United States,
Canada, and Mexico.

A native Californian presently living in McLean,
Virginia, Lunda received a Bachelor of Fine Arts degree

from Pomona College. She received her art training at the Art Students League in New York City and the Academia de Belli Arti in Florence, Italy.

The Smithsonian Institution's National Museum of Natural History held exhibitions of Lunda's paintings in 1976 and 1979. In 1978 and 1980 her work was exhibited by Hammer Galleries in New York City. Lunda's limited-edition silk screen prints are published by Hammer Graphics of New York. Selections from her works are reproduced in limited fine-art-edition prints and distributed throughout the United States by Frame House Gallery, Inc., Louisville, Kentucky.

Lunda has been featured on the national ABC television program "Good Morning, America," and the "Voice of America" and National Public Radio have broadcast special programs about her. Articles about her have appeared in *The Christian Science Monitor* and *People* magazine. She is included in *International Who's Who of Women* and *International Who's Who of Intellectuals.*

Lunda's work is included in the collections of Senator Henry Bellmon, Charlton Heston, Burt Reynolds, the Frye Museum of Seattle, New York's Genesee Country Museum, the Oklahoma Art Center, and various universities and other private collections throughout the world.

You may contact Lunda Hoyle Gill through Hammer Galleries, New York City, or by writing to 6931 River Oaks Dr., McLean, VA 22101, or telephoning (703) 893-2123.

IT STARTS WITH COMMITMENT

by LUNDA HOYLE GILL

Nothing is impossible. Nothing! Without commitment nothing can happen and never will. But make a commitment and your dreams will come true. It can happen to you just as it did to me.

On the wall of a friend's office are these framed words written by W. H. Murray: "Until one is committed there is hesitancy, the chance to draw back, always ineffectiveness. Concerning all acts of initiative and creation, there is one elementary truth—the moment one commits oneself, *providence moves too.*"

This is so true. Once a commitment is made, all kinds of things happen—unforeseen incidents, coincidental meetings, unexpected material assistance. They all play a part in helping you achieve your goal. Your projects, your desires, and your dreams suddenly begin to develop real-life substance.

I Make a Commitment

This happened to me. I was a successful portrait painter, but I was experiencing increasing dissatisfaction with my work. I felt that I was spinning my wheels, not growing, not developing. Yes, I had reached a plateau of success. But each day something inside me said this was not all that life held for me.

The feeling kept welling up until one day I said: "No more! No more portraits! I must change, I must reach out! I must take a chance and try something else. Even if I fail, I must try!" This was my hour of commitment. And it changed my life dramatically.

Right after I made that decision, fear crept in. What was I going to do? What was I going to paint? What did I have to say? Could I succeed in another form of art? I had felt that I was wasting my talent—now what was I to do with my ability?

Less than a week after I decided to change my work the self-fulfilling part of the commitment began. Providence moved, and unforeseen events began to happen to help me along my way.

I opened a *National Geographic* to an article on the Tasaday Tribe in the Philippines. Here, suddenly, was my answer: I would paint diverse cultures around the world. What love and beauty and innocence I saw in the faces of those natives! Immediately I longed to paint those people.

I realized that painting tribal peoples would satisfy my desire to do something worthwhile. Tribal cultures are now undergoing dramatic and accelerated change.

Native peoples are being studied and photographed by anthropologists, but recording these people in paint would give an additional dimension. By looking directly into the eyes of another human being and recording the feeling which passed between the two of us, I could capture something special. I could preserve an essential and fragile element of that culture.

Now I knew what I wanted to do. But how to do it? I started writing letters to the authorities seeking permission to visit the Tasaday Tribe. But in the meantime I was given another idea.

A dear artist friend, one of America's finest bird painters, had been working in Africa. His wife was captivated by the tribal peoples there and told me "Lunda, you must go to Africa and paint the people."

Instantly I made up my mind to do it. I did not even consider the problems involved in such an undertaking: the physical danger, the tremendous cost, the difficulty of securing local cooperation. Somehow I knew that I would do it, that I would manage, that it would happen.

A New Life

I was off on a new life! What exhilaration I felt, even though that fear was still beating in my breast. Would I fail? This was a whole new way of painting—would my paintings succeed? Would they be any good?

After taking care of all the detailed preparations I was finally off to Kenya. I was terrified. But all my fear vanished when my eyes drank in the beauty of the first person to pose for me. She was an old Kikuyu woman. Large distended holes in her earlobes held numerous beaded earrings. Her shaved head was decorated with a band of beads across the forehead, and she was wearing several intricately beaded necklaces. From that moment on I knew how I wanted to spend the rest of my life.

Since that trip to Africa I have traveled thousands of miles. I still haven't succeeded in visiting the Tasaday Tribe (I am still trying) but I have worked with Eskimos in Alaska, Aborigines in Australia, cannibals in Papua New Guinea, Margaret Mead's people in Bali, and American Indians in the United States. There have been countless exciting adventures. My commitment is paying me back a hundred-fold for what I have invested in it.

Three New Joys

Three main joys come out of my commitment. The first is that of looking deep into the eyes and soul of another person and using my paints to create life on a piece of blank, dead canvas. I can't begin to explain how I feel in the instant when my subject comes alive on the canvas and winks back at me. I get the same feeling from looking at Michelangelo's unfinished sculptures, his "stone slaves," in which one can actually see living, breathing men breaking out of the stone.

•

The second joy of my new work is the personal communication that it requires. I can only paint what I see and feel. In order for me to capture the real essence of the subject, that person must be open to me. So I try to establish a very special relationship with my subjects. This has permitted me to see more than just the outer façade of their skin, bone structure, hair color, and dress. I look beyond that to the people inside, but I cannot paint anything they do not give me.

Magic occurs between my sitters and me. They let me see inside their minds and hearts. They, like me, wish for the best possible paintings. They know their children and their future descendants will view these paintings in years to come.

Many of my subjects have told me stories about themselves which I know they have never told another living soul. They know instinctively that I will not betray their confidence. That's true—I couldn't. What they share with me is one of the greatest treasures of my work.

After spending four days with someone halfway around the world, I leave knowing that we have touched each other's lives with meaning that will last forever. This happens to me with each new person who honors me by agreeing to pose. And this giving renews me time and again and makes me work harder and stretch for the next adventure. Yes, my life is an adventure now.

•

My third great joy is communicating with other people through my paintings. Maybe this is what art is all about. I hope that when others view my paintings they will like my friends and feel a little closer to them by seeing through my eyes.

I would like to tell you about one of the remarkable individuals I have painted. I was stranded in Alaska on St. Lawrence Island off Siberia for four days when we were weathered in with fog and no plane could land. During that time I received much help and kindness from a Siberian Eskimo woman named Anna.

Anna must have been extraordinarily beautiful as a girl, because today, in her 70s, she is a rare beauty. On her face are etched beautiful geometric tattoos which were sewn there when she was 12 to 14 years old. The tattoos were sewn with sinew dipped in ashes, and the very same designs appear on ivory artifacts excavated by the Smithsonian Institution and carbon-dated to be more than 2,000 years old. Anna is a living artifact!

But her beauty is not only on the surface—it is deep within her, the inner beauty of a very special woman. I saw the look of years in her eyes, the look that only time is able to etch into a face. I saw there pain, happiness, the death of loved ones, the joy of giving birth, silent suffering from cold and hunger, the giving and receiving of love, and hard work—hour after hour, day after day, and year after year of work. All this flashed across her face in an instant.

Anna has lived on desolate St. Lawrence Island all of her life. Unlike most Eskimo women, Anna goes whaling with her husband. She does the same work the men do, and then she goes home and does her own work.

If you have ever seen a picture of the tiny skin boats the Eskimos use for whaling you would understand a little of Anna's courage. That water is so cold that if a boat should overturn it would mean instant death.

As I left the island Anna put her hand on my shoulder and said "Lunda, you have so honored me by being in my house!"

I couldn't speak, and it was hard for me to hold back my tears, for I knew that I was the honored one—she had allowed me to know her and paint her.

The day I left Alaska I felt the first winds of winter chill my bones, and I thought of Anna. I hoped the winter wouldn't be too hard on her. How does she survive? My admiration and respect will be with her always.

Help Came from Many

I told you that all kinds of unexpected assistance came my way as soon as I made a commitment. It happens that way. People go out of their way to help you when they realize that you are wholly serious and wholly committed to your goal. We all do a lot of talking without substance or conviction—our conversations are filled with words like *maybe, if, when,* and *possibly.* When a commitment is made these words change to *will, can, yes,* and *must.* The whole world changes then. When people take you seriously they want to help you. They become as excited as you about what you are doing.

Without all the help that I received from so many people I could never have produced even one painting. I wish to thank them now—they know who they are!

I have been given many different kinds of help. When I was painting Chippewa Cree Indians on the Rocky Boys Indian Reservation in Montana, I got caught in a blizzard. I had no food and no place to sleep. The Indians gave me a bed and fed me abundantly for four days. They got my car running again (at 20 degrees below zero!), and then, as I was leaving, they gave me a magnificent hand-made beaded belt. I will always treasure that belt and their friendship.

Margaret Mead, the great anthropologist, was very kind to me. She allowed me to meet with her in Bali, where she had done extensive work 40 years earlier. While I was there I painted her cook, her gardener, and her adopted son (who had been the model in her film about bathing babies 40 years ago). In part because of this experience I am now being called an ethnographic artist.

A Tari wigman in the highlands of Papua New Guinea was so happy with his painting that he sat in the rain all night to guard my hut so that no evil spirits could harm me. (I had painted him in a straw hut with no sides; only a roof held up by four poles kept off the rain.)

A Well-Calculated Risk

Another special plus that comes from making a commitment is that you become more courageous, bolder, more sure of yourself, and more ready to take necessary well-thought-out chances. Taking calculated risks is essential to winning.

One of my scariest, most exciting, and most rewarding adventures occurred because I went against official advice. That was a calculated risk. An Australian Aborigine chief had agreed to pose for me if I would come to his home in Arnhem Land. The night before I was to fly out from Darwin I received a telegram from an Australian government official advising me not to go.

A relative of the chief had died. Whereas no one is allowed on Aborigine land at any time without permission from the Aborigine council, only Aborigines may be present at Aborigine funerals, and these funerals go on for days.

I decided to go despite the government's warning. I had traveled halfway around the world already—why give up so easily? So I put my money down on the counter and bought my plane ticket for another adventure.

Not long after, I found myself following the chief's wife down to the beach where the funeral was being held. The chief couldn't come out, so he had requested that I come in. I felt very uneasy following that woman into the unknown land of an Aborigine funeral. What would those people think of me, with my blond hair and my left-handedness? Would they accept me, or would I seem like an evil spirit? If any one person took an instant dislike to me, my life would be in danger. I knew that I might be in serious trouble, but I had to go on.

What sights and sounds greeted me as I reached the mourners! The women wailed and lamented, swaying to and fro, while men played the haunting *didjeridu* and children ran all about. I had stepped into a world of 30,000 years ago!

I painted five pictures at that funeral, sitting in the

sand with my canvas propped against a rock.

Unexpected Rewards

An important element of commitment is the rewards it brings. When I went to Africa I never dreamed that less than two years later I would be cutting a blue ribbon in the Smithsonian Institution's National Museum of Natural History, opening a three-month exhibit of my African tribal paintings. Now, after my second exhibition there—this one of Alaska's native peoples, the Eskimos, the Aleuts, and the Indians—I still can't believe it's true!

During the Smithsonian exhibition, Frame House Gallery, Inc., of Louisville, Kentucky, published and distributed a fine-art limited-edition print of my painting of a Gabra man from northern Kenya. (I had found this man majestic, his face a beautiful leather, tanned from years of sun and wind. He radiated great inner strength derived from years in the desert with camel caravans. He will be forever imprinted on my mind.)

As a student at the Art Students League in New York City, I used to look longingly in the windows of Hammer Galleries, dreaming that someday my paintings would be there. Now Hammer Galleries publishes silk-screen prints of my paintings.

If I had not taken a chance and made a commitment, had I continued to sit and wait for something to happen in my life, I would still be waiting. I had to commit myself in order for my dreams to come true.

Braving the Crocodiles

Now that I have achieved some small fame as an artist and adventurer and my paintings command a worthy price, I am often asked if this accomplishment was difficult. It was, and it still is.

I would be remiss if I allowed you to think that it has been easy to achieve my dreams. Who would find it easy to leave a secure home and travel to remote areas with unknown dangers? But once I commit myself I find that I can do anything I have to.

I have showered with a poisonous green mamba snake, crossed crocodile-infested rivers at night in a dugout canoe, and faced a hungry lioness. I once visited with a tribe of people who three months before I arrived had speared a man to death. I spent four nights on an island off the Siberian coast, faced cannibals, suffered extremes of heat and cold, and was almost eaten alive by mosquitos, worrying all the while about catching malaria.

Sometimes the physical demands of fulfilling my commitment have been almost more than I could handle. Several times I have thought that the end of my life was near.

This happened once in Papua New Guinea, where the Chambri Lake men make beauty by placing hibiscus at just the right angle in their hair and other natives wear bird-of-paradise feather headdresses three feet tall.

A terrible storm blew up late one night while I was with some natives in a dugout canoe in the middle of a lake. We were lost on the lake for hours. We could not see the shore. There were no lights anywhere, and the heavy rain was beginning to sink the canoe. Crocodiles were gliding alongside, just waiting.

Finally a far-away flicker of light showed on the horizon and we paddled toward it, reaching the shore soaked and completely exhausted.

At times like these I say to myself "What am I doing here? Why not be safe and warm in my own bed at home?" But when I think ahead to the beauty I will see tomorrow, I know the answer. The minute my subject sits in front of me and I begin to paint—then all is well with my world. I wouldn't change my life for any other.

New Mountains to Climb

The satisfaction of fulfilling my commitment far out-weighs the difficulties I experience. I know that through my paintings I am communicating the life of diverse tribes to many people who have never seen them in person and will never have that opportunity. I am recording a way of life for future generations who will never be able to experience it.

Have you ever climbed a mountain and wondered what was on the other side? Have you ever reached the mountaintop, looked over, and discovered a new world stretched out before you? And then discovered that there were *more* mountains to climb, *more* fields to conquer, *more* beauty to discover? Without climbing that first mountain, you would have no way of knowing about the mountains, the beauties, the adventures yet to come.

Life is exactly like that—until we try, until we commit ourselves, stretch ourselves a little further, we are limited by what we have experienced. Only by reaching out can we touch our ultimate potential. This is the greatest point of total freedom—the conquering of ourselves.

It starts with commitment.

You can make a commitment now, today! Let me know if you do. I care.

DENNIS B. ADAMS

A speaker, motivator, and salesperson with more than ten years' experience as a family-and-marriage counselor, Dennis Adams knows the challenge of taking raw theories and applying them to the reality of day-to-day life.

In his work with disadvantaged youth, Dennis has overseen the operation of the San Francisco-based chapter of Youth Opportunities United and is currently secretary of the board of governors of the California Youth Development Foundation.

Dennis also serves on the board of directors of Continental Research and Development Corporation, a think-tank organization that engineers ideas through development and marketing stages.

He is no stranger to the lectern, as he has inspired and motivated hundreds of groups, including schools, clubs, churches, and charitable organizations. He has also conducted workshops on self-actualization and marriage-and-family relationships.

Currently director of author services for Showcase Publishing Company, Dennis is an active member of the Sales and Marketing Executives Association, the American Society for Training and Development, and the National Speakers Association.

You may contact Dennis by writing P.O. Box 41, Moss Beach, CA 94038, or by telephoning (707) 422-6822 or (415) 728-7186.

CREATIVE DISSATISFACTION

by DENNIS B. ADAMS

Oxford, England, 1954: Roger Bannister snaps the tape at the end of a mile run to accomplish what society-at-large deemed impossible. He has just run a mile in less than four minutes.

After Bannister broke the four-minute barrier, man redefined the parameters of his illusion. Many other runners were quick to follow, realizing that they, too, could have their names in the record books—and with even better times. The later successes, just like Bannister's, were due not to vitamins or some super exercise regimen (although diet and training did play a part), but to the impetus that originated between the champion's ears. This force was derived from the combination of a tangible goal with an ardent dissatisfaction—dissatisfaction with present performance.

It is a love-hate ambivalence that fuels the fires of success. Without a present and perhaps intense dissatisfaction to fan the flames, a goal remains nothing more than a dream. On the other hand, dissatisfaction unaccompanied by a goal or a dream often leads to deadly cynicism and bitterness.

Many barber-chair philosophers and Monday morning quarterbacks can pinpoint the world's problems or graphically demonstrate a coach's tactical errors. But lacking a definite goal of their own, they never advance beyond the barber chair or bar stool. I saw many examples of this in my counseling work in prisons. Some prisoners thought they knew the law better than any of the judges and lawyers who had worked to jail them. They knew exactly what laws had been bent to cause them to be unjustly detained.

I asked several of them, "If you know the law so well, why are you and the prosecuting attorney on opposite sides of the bars?"

These men were content to stew in their own dissatisfaction. Rather than select a goal to move toward, rather than build on their experience by studying courses that might eventually lead to a law degree, they sat back and replayed their own trials. In today's courtrooms there are a number of judges and lawyers who began their careers on the less desirable side of the bars. They are the select few who combined their grassroot dissatisfaction with a definable goal. Their initial failure became a springboard to success.

We have all encountered dreamers whose great plans descend upon us like a huge gaseous cloud without shape or form. Their legs aren't quite long enough for their feet to touch solid ground, and they never do discover a practical application for all their gilt-edged theory. These people need to isolate an area in their lives where they are dissatisfied and attach a few of their dreams to it. Dissatisfaction would provide the tangible substance that would enable them to accomplish something.

Listen to Your Dissatisfaction

Considering the tremendous importance of positive thinking, the concept of creative dissatisfaction might seem uncomfortably negative to some. Actually, the discomfort of dissatisfaction is a most positive aspect. Dissatisfaction is life itself counseling you about areas where you are running into conflict.

Placing one's hand on a hot stove is not comfortable, but we have to appreciate the positive value of our nerve endings' response. The pain gives warning before the damage is irreversible.

Some of our fastest marathon runners are able to excel by deliberately not tuning out their pain and discomfort. Instead they *focus on their pain* and make immediate adjustments to alleviate it. Not only do they eliminate the distraction of the pain, but they also avoid the bodily injuries which frequently result from the stress of competition. This is an example of how present dissatisfaction can be a guide to help us avoid more serious dissatisfaction in the future.

All of us have areas of dissatisfaction in our lives, and it is vital that we acknowledge them. Blinding our eyes will not cause our problem areas to disappear, and by denying reality we may be cutting ourselves off from a source of positive energy.

The potential energy inherent in dissatisfaction is illustrated by the story of a young man in search of truth who consults an aged philosopher. The two of them go to the shore, and together they wade into the water. When the water is about waist deep, the sage plunges the youth below the surface and holds him there, despite his wild thrashing to get free.

When at last the old man lets the youth come sputtering up, the youth cries: "Why did you do that to me? All I did was ask you a simple question concerning where I might find truth, and you tried to drown me!"

"I was merely illustrating a point," replies the old gentleman. "When you desire truth the same way you just desired a breath of fresh air, you will find it."

That young man did not lie back and think to himself: "I sure wish I could have some air. I just don't know why it is that other people have more air than I do—it's just not fair! Oh well, I guess that's the way it is—some people just seem to have all the luck!"

No, the youth's dissatisfaction with drowning moved him to immediate action toward a tangible goal. It boosted his energy level to the point where he could not do otherwise.

Where in your life are you unable to breathe? And what are you doing about it? When your dissatisfaction reaches a level where there is no longer a choice, it will become a simple matter for you to go forward, to press on toward a solution. The more skilled you are at identifying areas of dissatisfaction in your life, the more you will save yourself from future hurt.

Use Dissatisfaction as a Spur

Creative dissatisfaction can be a positive tool in overcoming problems because it reduces fear of failure. Once you realize that you are not succeeding in some area, it also becomes evident that failing in the attempt to remedy the problem will result in your ending up in no worse state than when you started.

A popular illustration of fear of failure involves a challenge to walk a plank for a $10 reward. If the plank were lying on the ground, we could all easily walk its length. But with the plank at a height of 20 stories, fear of failure will divert our attention from achieving our goal.

Now let's put a hungry lion on the roof, leaving the plank as the only means of escape. Now fear of future failure is reduced; we are *already* in a condition of failure unless we act quickly. When we walk the plank we won't be longing to be back where we started—we will be eager to be safely on the other side. Our attention will be more sharply focused on achieving our goal.

If we each could place a pot of gold in front of us and a lion behind us, we would be virtually assured of achieving success! Yet, if we view reality in the proper perspective, we all have pots of gold in front and lions behind. The lions are our areas of acute dissatisfaction, and the pots of gold are whichever riches we wish to attain.

This approach has been implemented many times in history by famous leaders. Caesar, who burned his bridges behind him as he crossed the Rubicon, and Cortez, who set fire to his ships after landing at Veracruz, both gave their men the choice of struggling for that breath of air or drowning. Do or die—fight or perish!

When one leaves an area of dissatisfaction, one is not so tempted to look back. There is no comfortable back door to look to, but, rather, charred ruins. That knowledge makes one press on with renewed determination.

I used creative dissatisfaction to achieve a goal when I moved to California. I felt that if one lived in California, one should live on the beach. Unfortunately I was not the first person to reach this conclusion. The real estate values of coastal property were astronomical. The largest down payment I could manage would barely bring a condescending smile to the face of an area realtor.

After several months of dogged, if not sometimes dispirited, determination, I managed to secure a small piece of property commanding a beautiful view of the ocean. It did have a few drawbacks: it was an empty lot, there were no streets, and the land was located wthin the regulated Coastal Commission Zone, the Geologic Hazard Zone, the Airport Advisory Zone, and the Environmental Impact Study Zone. At the same time, the country was in a recession and construction money was almost non-existent—if one could qualify—and I could not.

With all of these factors to deal with, I realized that now was the time to breathe life into my old dream of designing and constructing my own home in my spare time. There was the goal. The dissatisfaction came partly from the reaction of friends and relatives familiar with my background. They were certain that I would fail and become an embarrassment to them and the community. (Who was it who told Bannister he couldn't break the four-minute mile?)

I generated more dissatisfaction by moving my wife, my two children, an unhousebroken puppy, and a canary into a nearby 80-year-old one-bedroom rental cottage until such time as I could get our house built. "It will draw us together," I told my dubious wife.

As I watched my books mildew and our stacked furniture slowly succumb to the elements, my need to accomplish was fanned to a modest flame. And as I sat at the kitchen table drawing and redrawing blueprints to the sounds of our dog, canary, and kids, that flame became a white-hot torch. One day soon I would hear instead the crashing sound of ocean waves.

In just one year, with dissatisfaction as a spur, I unraveled the bureaucratic red tape of financing, plan approval, and multi-commission approval; and in the next year, with hardened muscles and blackened fingernails, I was sitting on the third-story deck of my new home overlooking a 200-degree panoramic view of the Pacific!

I had learned a valuable lesson: dissatisfaction transformed into satisfaction can be incalculably rewarding, and the process is a source of self-sustaining energy. Once one has walked the plank and is safe on the other side, it is a great joy to look back at the leering face of the lion. Planks are transformed from obstacles to challenges, and one learns to look forward to the next contest.

•

Now that we have moved into the new house, it is amazing how long the final finish-work has taken! The dissatisfaction has subsided. Someday I'm going to finish that house. But today I have more important things to do—such as watching a beautiful sunset. When the dissatisfaction goes, the catalytic force goes too. Then one may once again be like a slack sail on a windless day.

•

The word *creative* is very important when describing this approach to problem solving. Focusing on dissatisfaction of itself and by itself, without introducing creativity, can lead to negativism, and the personal analysis can become a negative, self-fulfilling prophecy.

To use dissatisfaction creatively a person must:

1. Face the real problem.
2. Evaluate the urgency of doing something.
3. Select a goal that will solve the problem.
4. Follow a plan to accomplish that goal.

Face the Problem

Many outstanding successes are achieved in spite of numerous obstacles and discouraging odds. Pete Strudwick, the author of a chapter in Volume 4 of this series, could have allowed a severe physical handicap to prevent him from meeting his life goals. Strudwick was born without feet, yet he trained himself to run the Pike's Peak Marathon, and his victory over his handicap carried him into national prominence.

Obstacles in your life can present the same success-generating challenge. You can face them squarely and take them on in the battlefield of everyday living, or you can make them a convenient excuse for remaining a non-achiever.

Examining an area of dissatisfaction is not a negative reflection on you as a person. We look at the dissatisfaction simply to define the problems. Then we are faced with a basic question: "Am I willing to tolerate this problem, even though it will continue to dissipate my energy in a negative direction, or am I going to act to overcome it?"

Once you see yourself with all your pluses and minuses, you will be in a good position to choose where you want to go from there. What are you content to live with? How many personal four-plus-minute miles are you willing to accept in your life? And which areas are you ready to change?

You will find areas that you are not ready or willing to act on yet. That's fine—leave them alone for now, but know that they are dormant not because you are afraid to face them, but because your self-determined priorities dictate that another area be tackled first.

You also have areas that are not satisfying to you but which, at the same time, are not keeping you from being happy. Nobody is going to achieve perfection in this life. Each of us has to face the fact that there are certain things we will not be able to overcome or accomplish. Decide what you are willing to tolerate, at least for the time being, and what to put on the agenda to be changed.

Putting your dissatisfaction to creative use means refusing to allow the negative areas in your life to sit in the driver's seat. Don't let circumstance steer your future course.

Evaluate the Urgency

Once you have isolated an area of dissatisfaction in your life, ask yourself, "How intensely do I dislike this area?"

Every alcoholic dislikes being an alcoholic. The problem lies in the fact that the alcoholic does not dislike it as much as he likes it! Dissatisfaction has not reached the level of intensity where it is an automatic motivator toward a positive goal.

At some time or other everyone has fantasized about being a professional athlete, a political figure, a television personality, or some other highly visible success model. But unless you have been dissatisfied enough to invest the intense effort required to develop such a career path, you are still fantasizing. Usually it is a lot more pleasant and satisfying to do a less demanding job and spend one's extra time enjoying life.

Every salesperson would like to make more money, but many lack enough present dissatisfaction to get through those hardest of all doors to open—the front door to leave for work, and the car door to begin the day's sales. Then, when the month's quota has been met, are they dissatisfied enough with their present record to continue making cold calls and resurrecting old leads and referrals? Or, because the heat is off, do they slacken their pace?

How does this correlate with the way you function in your career field? Are you willing to consistently expend more effort than is required to get by? You may feel that it is better to lead a more balanced life—less work and more play. That's fine *so long as you are willing to accept that you will wind up living with less money.* The choice is yours to make. The important thing is that you do make a conscious choice! If you are not spending your life for something, you will end up spending it for nothing.

If you are satisfied now with punching the time clock in a secure job situation, don't feel cheated when 20 or 30 years from now you are retired with a handshake and a gold Timex.

•

The salesperson who dislikes making cold calls may decide that discomfort in this area is a necessary dissatisfaction. Wanting to continue in sales, and in fact, wanting to become more successful, this salesperson can make use of present dissatisfaction as a motivator to learn more about the product, to formulate smooth answers to questions and objections, to attend sales seminars, and to read books written by successful salespeople. More knowledge and new ideas may result in a more professional, confident, and successful manner of handling the cold call.

All jobs have areas of necessary dissatisfaction—routine, boring, or distasteful functions which must be performed. One needs to examine whether doing that disliked task is more onerous than the inevitable result of not doing it. A salesperson who hates cold calls should consider the inevitable result of avoiding them: cold calls are far less dissatisfying than financial ruin, job hunting, and going hungry!

This mental exercise of considering the ultimate end can help one realize that an important part of achieving anything worthwhile is hard work and self-discipline. Not every workout is a joy, but no athlete who wants to win can afford to miss one.

It is possible, however, that this same salesperson may conclude that cold calls are an intolerable dissatisfaction. This is a case where dissatisfaction signals an urgent need for change. It could be used creatively for motivation to explore other career opportunities. If you cannot cope with the areas of dissatisfaction essential to your job, you owe it to yourself to find another job. Not only will you be happier, but you will perform better.

Select the Right Goal

It takes wisdom to connect present dissatisfaction with a goal that will truly solve the problem. Everyone has plenty of dissatisfaction, but not many hitch it to a goal that will bring them lasting fulfillment. A disadvantaged youth may see quick easy money as a simple solution to his aching poverty. Later he may discover that he has added a prison record to his list of liabilities.

Most of us wish we were better liked and more respected by others. We also harbor feelings of inferiority and low self-esteem. These areas can provide a prolific ground-base of present dissatisfaction to fire up our boilers with the energy for achieving our goals, but selecting the right goal is crucial.

In my experience as a marriage-and-family counselor I have observed great unhappiness in many families. Frequently there is a father who years ago sought high position in his business or profession. He chose that goal in order to ease his own inner dissatisfaction—reasoning that money could buy happiness.

But achieving the position he wanted and the salary that went along with it required much time and energy.

Making it in the business world left little time for father-
ing. And you can't make up to a child for that loss of
support and patterning with a super trip to Disneyland, a
bicycle, or a car at age 16.

All too often the dissatisfied children tried to fill
their own vacuums at the over-supplied family liquor
cabinet or turned to spending their liberal allowances on
a plethora of hallucinogenic drugs.

What do you choose to hitch your dissatisfaction to?
We joke about the ladder of success being crowded at the
bottom, but it is also very lonely at the top.

If you decide that cold cash is the answer to all your
needs, you might consider that, even when viewed from a
cold-cash philosophy, it pays to give time and energy to
your family. It costs much less to keep one's mate happy
than to pay alimony to several "ex's"! Time propitiously
shared with a child is vastly more economical than paying fees to lawyers and psychiatrists later.

●

All too often we are told what our goals should be. Yet
what society calls success may not be success for everyone. I knew a person who had achieved great status in the
computer industry but was dissatisfied with his life. To
him, the ideal lifestyle was similar to what Neil Diamond portrays in his song "Forever in Blue Jeans."

My friend longed to trade in his three-piece business
suits and corporate pressures for a less formal life. He
eventually resigned from his company and bought an
auto-wrecking yard.

For most people, working in an auto-wrecking yard
would represent anything but success. Yet this man and
his family are very happy. He had climbed the ladder to
what society calls success, only to find that the ladder
was leaning against the wrong wall. By taking a realistic

look at the dissatisfactions in your life and examining what is making you unhappy, you can better determine what you need for happiness.

Follow a Plan

Critical examination of the areas of dissatisfaction in your life will reveal the priorities that lead toward your individual success. Decide what is most important in your life and what can be compromised.

As the first step in formulating a life plan, ask yourself these questions:

1. How important is geography: Where do you want to live and how much is it worth to you? Are you willing to settle for less money to live in the rolling hills of Kansas?

2. What gives you satisfaction and fulfillment: Is it completing a project, having others consider you dependable, interacting with others, or working with your hands?

3. What kind of money do you realistically need: What are your plans for retirement? Are you willing to take risks, or do you desire the security of a pension?

4. What about physical environment: Would you rather work traditional hours or a floating schedule? Do you prefer an informal or a formal structure? What type of clothing would you like to wear to work? How much space do you need?

5. What about people: Do you prefer a company of ten or a company of 10,000? How closely do you want to work with associates? Are you an independent, who likes to work alone? Do you prefer the public or private sector?

6. What kinds of skills and knowledge do you want to use on the job: mechanical, verbal, mathematical, idea-related, musical, educational?

7. What level of responsibility satisfies you: Do you want to be the manager or part of the team?

This list is meant to be a catalyst to your own thinking. It is well worth taking the time to complete the process with questions that are relevant to your life.

•

Assuming that you have now examined your life, you have discovered areas which make you unhappy and which you are unwilling to tolerate. You are looking at a lot of potentially positive energy just waiting to be put to use. The next step is to visualize yourself stepping out and overcoming or circumventing that dissatisfaction.

If you were an athlete who was dissatisfied with the progress you had made thus far, perhaps the time required for you to run the mile, you would combine your dissatisfaction with a visualization of success. You would picture in your mind's eye the vivid moment of accomplishing your goal. You would see yourself breaking the tape, victorious, coming in first with a record time. Visualizing yourself achieving what you have set out to do is a proven success formula.

Find Your Motivation

Many people think of motivation as some kind of external, consumable energy source. They want to know where the gas pump is for filling their empty tank. In reality, each of us *already has* motivation. Rather than asking where to get it, we should examine *where motivation already exists within us,* and then learn how to channel it in a more productive way.

Have you ever taken note of the enormous supply of energy radiated at a disco dance? The person who is dancing with such enthusiastic abandon may be the same person who was barely able to summon up the strength to function at work only a few hours earlier!

I observed this same phenomenon in the South Pacific, where it was too hot and humid for the young islanders to work at midday. But just let someone appear on the scene with a soccer ball, and the torrid tropical heat was quickly forgotten.

Anyone who has watched children play can appreciate the value of harnessing all that play motivation into work motivation. Bill Cosby says, "Give me 200 kids under the age of six and I can conquer the world!"

To harness your own motivational energy you need only to pinpoint the source of your negative energy flow. It's where your greatest dissatisfaction lies. (If you wonder where your get-up-and-go done got-up-and-went—that's where!) And that is where your energy will continue to dissipate until you set out on a plan of positive change. A small amount of negative energy can offset a large amount of positive energy; a little leavening raises the whole lump.

When we decide to take action, we can utilize the energy that has been draining away and funnel it in a positive direction. This is the technique Howard Jarvis utilized in organizing California residents to push through legislation to reduce property taxes. He focused on the public's dissatisfaction with their state government and the tax structure and offered them a solution, a goal, to strive for.

Some people may argue that Jarvis offered the wrong solution, but his impetus came from widespread public dissatisfaction. He capitalized on it and re-engineered it. If everyone had been satisfied with the tax structure and leadership in the state, Jarvis would not have had a platform to stand on.

•

In our own lives the problem areas have a way of becoming habitualized. They will not automatically heal themselves. The old adage "As soon as I can get some heat out of this stove, then I'll throw some wood in," applies here. When you focus on your dissatisfaction enough to realize how very cold it is, then you will be willing to go out and chop wood, gather it up to stoke the fire, and blow on the kindling until the warmth of the flame satisfies your needs and desires.

Your dissatisfaction will always be there, whether or not you acknowledge its existence. Why not capitalize on it and use it creatively? Make it a tool for building a better you!

TOM HAWKES

Tom Hawkes was born in Tulare, California, but received most of his education, including trade, business, and engineering courses, in the East and Midwest.

A graduate of the Air University's Air Command and Staff School, Tom spent 12 years in the Air Force as a pilot during WWII and the Korean War.

He has been a senior industrial engineer, a chief industrial engineer, and has owned a contracting business. During the past ten years he has been a consultant to business and government.

For seven years Tom was the producer and speaker on the daily syndicated radio commentary, "American Heritage." He is the author of a philosophical history of the United States and has written numerous articles for newspapers and periodicals.

Tom is a widely accepted speaker on motivation and self-help in the communications field, and has given many talks and seminars for businesses and organizations. He has been a member of Toastmasters International for 28 years and is a current member of the International Platform Association.

Tom Hawkes can be reached by writing to him at 1363 Ballena Boulevard, Alameda, CA 94501; or by telephoning (415) 865-5691.

GET ON THE RIGHT WAVELENGTH!

by TOM HAWKES

All of us, whether openly or in secret, like to think of ourselves as good communicators. We all like to be solid citizens who stand up and are counted whenever the need arises. We attend public meetings such as church groups, the local PTA, the city council, or some federal hearing. We stand up on the floor or before the microphone and "tell it like it is." We can make a sales presentation that no one can refuse. We are the top conversationalist at any party. Right? WRONG!

Most of us would like to be that kind of communicator. Most of us *dream* about being that kind of communicator. Unfortunately, most of us are living proof of the statement, "The greatest enemy of communication is the illusion that it has already happened."

How many times have you said "I wish I'd said that?" How many times have you prepared yourself to go to bat publicly for some cause and then either sat silent when the time came, or got up only to stutter, stammer, and struggle through your presentation, knowing full well that you were convincing no one?

Well, if you are one of the millions of people in this category, I've got news for you! *You can do it!* You can be the kind of communicator that you've always dreamed about! This is not to say that you will always win every battle and always convince people of your viewpoint. But you can be a communicator to whom people will listen, a respected communicator who will be called on more and more frequently to offer opinions and to lead others.

Oral and written communications are somewhat like a two-way radio. Before one radio can transmit to another, it must be on the right wavelength. As a communicator, you must be on the same wavelength as your listeners, or they will receive nothing but a lot of static. Similarly, if your listeners are not tuned in, your message will fall on empty space.

The Four Basics

How does one get on the right communications wavelength? There are four basic ingredients for good communicating. Anyone can improve communications skills by developing desire and self-discipline, doing some homework, and then going into action. Let's take a look at these four components.

1. *Desire.* We've said that almost everyone wants to be a good communicator, but just wanting to is not enough. One must have a positive desire to communicate.

Sometimes it takes a little self-analysis to find your real desire. It helps to listen to yourself talk. Perhaps you've said the same things to yourself on numerous occasions: "My wife doesn't understand me." "My boss doesn't know that I exist." "What's the use of going to that meeting? No one ever listens." "Somehow, I've got to make them understand!"

Are they familiar words? Sure they are. These are just some of the common everyday communication failures that we all experience. If these everyday situations were crises, however, you would somehow manage to make yourself clearly understood. Your desire to communicate would then be so strong that you would find the right wavelength to deliver an effective message.

Consider that, by taking steps to improve your communication now, you may prevent daily experiences from developing into crises. Now wouldn't that be worthwhile? When you add purpose to simple wants, you have desire. Desire is a powerful motivator. Think about the marvelous relationships you can initiate and maintain, the fun you can have, and the good will you can create, if you have the desire to communicate well.

2. *Self-discipline.* Every commission salesperson, entrepreneur, independent businessperson, consultant, or professional knows that the key to success is self-discipline. One must be able to govern one's own thoughts, actions, and time in order to succeed. Even people who work by the hour, week, or month need self-discipline to move up the ladder.

I remember when I was an industrial engineer working for a multi-national corporation and evaluation time came around. All of us received raises or promotions except one junior engineer. He went to the director of engineering and asked what was wrong. The director told him, "You haven't engineered!"

The young man was astounded and asked what the director meant. The director answered, "Son, you are an adequate engineer. Your knowledge is acceptable and you perform your job in a routine manner. However, part of any engineering discipline is to be able to create things. A new method. A new machine. An improvement here or there. So far, you have not offered anything new. You just haven't 'engineered!' There are lots of new ideas out there. You need to learn to discipline yourself to always be on the lookout for them."

You, too, have to learn and practice self-discipline. You have to learn how to get on the right wavelength and force yourself to practice until it becomes a habit.

Maybe you are saying, "I'm no good at self-discipline! I just can't force myself into routines!"

Well how about those weekly arguments with your husband or wife? Or those monthly "dressing-downs" because you didn't make your quota? Or those boring hours on the job, day after day? The meetings you didn't attend and the successes you just didn't have? These are all routines. They are routines you've brought on yourself and allowed to become habits.

It's just as easy to establish good habits as to suffer from bad ones. And good habits bring rewards instead of reprimands. Get started now on developing good habits. Pick out just one area at a time and get on the right wavelength with a new good habit.

3. *Homework.* Perhaps you thought you were all through with homework when you left school! Nevertheless, all successful people, from businesspeople to politicians and administrators, continue to do homework. We could also call it *research on the project at hand.* High school and college taught us where to go to look things

up. *Use* those research skills! Knowledge is both power and strength. (Remember, "Forewarned is forearmed!")

Imagine that you've come up with a new process for production in your manufacturing plant. Your project has gained the approval of your immediate supervisor and has passed a review committee. You have now been asked to present your ideas to the executive committee.

Homework is in order. You should research answers to such questions as: Who are the people on the executive committee? What are they like? What divisions of the organization do they represent? What are the likes and dislikes of each member? What philosophies do they follow?

You can find answers to all of these questions by some discreet observations, a few questions, and a look at the minutes and records of the corporation. A day or so of research should give you the answers. Then, when you make your presentation, you will be able to direct it to each individual's area of interest. You have improved your chances of acceptance by 80 percent!

For another hypothetical example, suppose you want to change jobs. You have a tentative offer, but you know that your spouse is very happy with your present situation and has been making plans around it. How should you go about winning your partner's support?

First of all, you should understand exactly what your partner wants and why. You can learn this through conversation. Once you understand your partner's feelings and goals, you should be able to point out ways that your job change could be an advantage. By doing your homework, you can come up with points that are positive from the other person's position.

By now you can probably think of many varied situations in which to do background research. Knowledge of past developments and of participants' reactions to similar situations will help you to present a case which others can understand, and which can be made to seem logical and positive to them. Moreover, if you have all the facts and conditions at hand, you will have infinitely more confidence in your presentation.

4. *Action.* Nothing ever happens until someone does something! If you don't do it, then someone else will, and nine times out of ten the results will not be favorable to you. More military, political, and philosophical defeats are sustained by the apathy of the defeated than by the brilliance of the victors.

It has been said that bad governments are instituted by people who do nothing.

So how do you get started? Well, if you have the desire, and you've been able to discipline yourself to do the necessary homework, then just *jump in and get your feet wet!* Go to the hearing on the new city ordinance and have your say! Get some facts and figures together and tell them what you think!

You may not make many points at first, but little-by-little you'll be heard, listened to, and you'll win your case! You'll acquire the habit of sending messages on a wavelength that people will tune in to. You'll find it easier to convince people of your point of view. (None of this will occur, of course, if you never start!)

Many authors in this series have noted that failure is the hallmark of most successful people. This is true. Many of our greatest inventors, engineers, statesmen, and politicians started out only to fail—not once, but many times! They kept coming back, and eventually, they made it.

Sir Winston Churchill was one of the more famous failures in history. His parents were told that he might as well not attend school because he would never be able to achieve anything! He was about 60 years old when he became successful. Then, even after losing the post-World War II elections, he made a comeback four years later and became prime minister again.

What was Churchill's secret? *He did something!* Time and again, he got involved. Churchill is not a bad model for you to copy.

Learn How To Compromise

When you understand the four basics and are ready to go into action, it will be useful to know some specific procedures for making group presentations. One important element of arguing a position is being prepared with alternative plans, appropriate compromises.

As almost everyone knows, compromise is what makes this country of ours tick. Almost every law passed by Congress and the various state legislatures is a compromise measure.

Now compromise doesn't mean that principles are thrown out the window. Not at all! To gain acceptance by giving up everything you stand for is not winning, and it is not compromise—it is quitting! However, you must face each situation realistically. Always ask yourself this question: Is it better to put across *part* of my plan, or to have *none* of it accepted?

You will usually conclude that it is best to set a primary goal of having your full proposal accepted, then a second and, perhaps, even a third goal for varying degrees of partial acceptance. Let's see how this might work in practice.

You are a real estate broker. Your city planning and zoning commission has prepared a "no-growth" ordinance for the city which would place a five-year moratorium on multiple dwelling units in the city. It would also seriously restrict residential building by requiring five-acre minimum lot sizes. The ordinance is now ready for action by the city council.

It dawns on you that your business will be seriously impaired if the ordinance is passed. How do you proceed in opposing the ordinance?

First, you do research. What effect will this ordinance have on the total community? How much will the tax base dwindle and the current residents' taxes rise? How many jobs will be lost in business and industry? How many small businesses may fail? Will the schools and libraries lose supporting funds? Will new industry reject the city because it lacks housing for potential employees?

Once you have all the fact and figures, put them into a simple report that the average person can read and understand. Send a copy report to each of the city council members, the city clerk, and the city attorney. Then call the city clerk and ask to be included on the speakers' agenda of the next council meeting.

When the meeting night arrives, get to the meeting early! Watch people as they come in. Introduce yourself to as many council members as you can. When the room is about filled, or just before the meeting is about to begin, stand up and look around. Stand up long enough so the audience can have a good look at you. When it's time for you to speak, you will no longer be a total stranger, nor will you suddenly be faced with a sea of strange faces.

Before you speak, try to determine whether your supporters are in the majority or the minority. Find out where the council members stand. Now you are ready.

If you find that your supporters are in the majority and that the council is about even or slightly favoring your position, you will have a good chance of succeeding if you try to stop the ordinance completely.

On the other hand, if the opposition seems to be in the majority and the council is split or leaning to the opposition, then you should consider your first or second alternatives, such as modifying the ordinance to allow some limited growth and a one-acre minimum lot size. There are any number of modifications that you could prepare in advance to cover a variety of situations.

If the opposition is very heavy, you could ask the council to table the ordinance until a future date to allow some study.

This same general procedure can be used at almost any meeting, gathering, or conference. Variations of this approach can be used even in a person-to-person encounter. But, whatever you do, make sure that you take the time to "set the stage," so that you will be on the same wavelength as those with whom you are trying to communicate.

Keep It Simple

Now let's discuss some general rules about your presentations. The first is to keep it simple. This is an absolute must. Except for a few spokesmen and one or two others who are deeply involved with the matter at hand, most people will be turned off by complicated reports and statistics.

Make sure that what you have to say can be understood quickly and easily by your audience. Long sentences, complicated explanations, and redundancy can make you lose your audience in a hurry. I once heard a speaker who was considered a genius in his field. He was vice president and treasurer of a national union. He began his talk, and within five minutes 500 people were comfortably asleep!

His speech was deeply intellectual and his presentation was dry, dull, and complete with complicated statistics. Despite the quality of the audience, which included many individuals with masters and Ph.D. degrees, the speaker couldn't hold them. He had neglected to keep it simple.

On the same program, as a fun break, was an entertainer who gave an entire lecture of engineering doubletalk. Nothing he said made sense, and none of his charts and props made sense, yet he was a fantastic speaker. He held his audience spellbound for more than an hour. (Some people were even taking notes!)

When the put-on was revealed there were a few sheepish looks while the audience howled with laughter. *The manner of presentation, not the topic, is what counts.*

Tell the Truth!

The second and perhaps most important rule is to tell the truth at all times. While complexity will bore your audience, if you resort to lies, half-truths, and vague generalities, you will completely lose them. Unfortunately, many people infringe on credibility. They falsely assume that manipulating the truth will help to put their points across.

Make sure of your facts and figures. If you are going to use statistics as part of your presentation, use easily-proven "hard" statistics, which are a matter of general record and have been demonstrated by test and measurement or the passage of time.

"Soft" statistics are based on any number of variables and may differ according to the source used. (This kind of statistic can make you especially vulnerable to your opposition, because both sides can use them as arguments for their case.)

An example of a hard statistic is the number of people employed in this country at any given time. This figure comes from government records and reports kept by employers. The number of unemployed, however, is a soft statistic. Any number of variables are used by different agencies to identify the unemployed, and the figure is not readily verifiable.

Use of generalities is another trap into which a speaker can fall. *Approximately, about,* and *around* are words that can get you into nothing but trouble, yet many speakers are fond of them.

Sometimes the unembellished truth seems dull, but you can always present it in colorful and easily understood language. Abraham Lincoln was a colorful and truthful speaker. The opening words of his Gettysburg Address grabbed the audience's attention and told them the absolute truth at the same time: "Four score and seven years ago . . ." That is exactly 87 years, and that was exactly what Lincoln meant, but his choice of words helped to make a great speech. Do as he did: avoid generalities, spruce up your phraseology, use unusual words, but always *tell the truth!*

If you speak regularly, from time to time you will meet up with hecklers and zealots who will use every plan and trick known to upset you and your arguments. What can you do about them? Frankly, very little. The greatest virtues in such a situation are patience and a nice big smile! They will usually bring the audience to your side.

I know that it is extremely hard to smile and have patience in the midst of a heated debate. But remember your desire, self-discipline, homework, and action. You wanted to have your say. You've used self-discipline to do it. You've done your homework and you are putting on a good presentation. Now patience and a big smile will keep you on the right wavelength.

ROBERT L. MONTGOMERY

Robert L. Montgomery is internationally known as a consultant, speaker, and trainer specializing in communication, public speaking, memory, sales, and listening skills. He conducts courses for all levels of management, and, during the past 25 years, has taught more than 150,000 men and women from more than 50 countries.

He is president of R. L. Montgomery & Associates, Inc., in Burnsville, Minnesota. His clients include Corning Glass Works, American International Group, Textron, Blue Cross, Deutsch Electronics, Ingersoll-Rand, Jones and Laughlin Steel Corporation, Upjohn Company, and A.T.&T.

Mr. Montgomery has served as a consultant, trainer, and speaker for the American Management Association since 1969 and has been a principal speaker for the man-

211

agement course for eight years. He is also a chairman for courses in the General Management Division, the Human Resources Division, and the Presidents Association. He has conducted courses in public speaking and "Train the Trainer" at AMA for ten years. For the past three years he has taught a course in public speaking for presidents only.

A pioneer in training with videotape, Mr. Montgomery has written and recorded tapes and films for 3M, National Life of Vermont, Whirlpool, West Chemical Company, and Savings and Loan Foundation. American Management Association produced his best-selling audio-cassette series "Effective Speaking for Managers," "Memory Made Easy," and "Listen Your Way to Success." Audio Recording Company of California produced his newest audio-cassette package, "How To Sell in the 1980s: The Quick and Easy Way."

His first book, *A Master Guide to Public Speaking*, Harper & Row, was chosen by Macmillan Publishing Company as a 1979 Book-of-the-Month selection. His second book, *Memory Made Easy*, was released in June 1979 by AMACOM.

Mr. Montgomery majored in communication arts at Notre Dame, Catholic University in Washington, D.C., and the University of Wisconsin; and in psychology at Pace University in New York City. He has earned numerous awards for his speaking and teaching skills as well as for journalistic excellence and for community leadership and service to youth.

Mr. Montgomery is listed in *Who's Who in America*, the *Dictionary of International Biography*, and *Community Leaders of America*.

You can contact Robert Montgomery by writing R. L. Montgomery & Associates, Inc., 12313 Michelle Circle, Burnsville, Minn. 55337 or telephoning (612) 894-1348.

THE MAGIC
OF YOUR PERSONALITY

by R. L. MONTGOMERY

Money isn't everything.
I always wanted a good personality.

This confession was made by J. Paul Getty, regarded as the richest man in the world when he died in 1976. Imagine—billions of dollars in the bank and he couldn't buy what he wanted most!

A winning personality is priceless. And yet it is something we all can attain: we can develop our personalities. The great baseball player Satchel Paige believed that. His philosophy was "Nobody can help being born common, but ain't nobody got to remain ordinary."

Personality consists of distinctive qualities or characteristics. It is the sum total of our habits, skills, and attitudes reflected in our own unique self-expression. It includes character, speech, image, facial expression, and body expression.

That's what personality is, but the question is, how do you polish that personality? After all, nobody wants to be a diamond in the rough!

It all starts with your attitude. In a sentence, *you're not what you think you are, but what you think, you are.* If your attitude is right, your personality will be right.

William James, the father of American psychology, said: "Human beings can alter their lives by altering their attitudes of mind." Alter your thoughts and your attitudes and you can alter your life.

Marcus Aurelius said it centuries ago: "Our life is what our thoughts make it."

And in more recent times, Associate Justice of the Supreme Court Oliver Wendell Holmes declared: "Success is the result of our mental attitude; and the right mental attitude will bring results in everything you undertake."

Our society is based on the conviction that there are extraordinary possibilities in ordinary people. Each of us is unique. Each of us is one-of-a-kind. There never was and never will be anyone just like you! Geneticists claim that if you had 300 billion brothers and sisters, not one of them would be exactly like you.

My principal work for the last 25 years has been conducting courses in personality development for women and men, young and old, from all walks of life. I have trained more than 150,000 people in more than 50 countries. The ideas I share with you now were gained in the course of these training experiences.

Develop a positive outlook. It's important to develop a positive outlook, and it's an easy thing to do. First, associate with positive-thinking, positive-acting individuals. Keep away from negative colleagues or friends and neighbors who are constantly complaining, carping, and tearing down. They'll pull you down to their level.

Second, read positive books. Find them at the library, in book stores, and even on paperback book racks in drug, department and grocery stores. Read the classics: *The Power of Positive Thinking, Wake Up and Live, I Dare You, The Magic of Believing, Think and Grow Rich,* and the Bible. These bestsellers will keep you optimistic, positive, and vital.

Third, buy some cassettes on success and positive action by the top professionals in the fields of motivation, human relations, sales, and communication. It's always cheaper to learn from other people's experience. You can listen to the voices of top successful personalities on the tape deck in your car, and you can take a cassette player with you anywhere you go. Use the tape recorder to practice your own spoken delivery.

Fourth, join a Toastmasters International Club and learn how to listen, think and speak more effectively. It will cost you about $30 a year to affiliate with the organization in your area and start sharpening your personality among executive men and women. You'll be hooked into a high-wire society, and the fellowship alone will more than reward you for your time and effort.

Write to Toastmasters International, Santa Ana, CA 92711 for more information.

Those four steps will help you to move ahead fast in developing your mind, speech, and spirit. (Remember that the largest room in the world is the room for self-improvement!)

Use your voice. Two of the suggestions I have already given have to do with the voice. Your voice is the main extension of yourself, so it will pay you to develop a well-modulated voice and an articulate speaking style. Practice speaking as often as you can—by yourself, with your family, in a speech club, in meetings and conferences at work, or wherever you have the opportunity. Practice is the best instructor.

People who dazzle others with witty conversation, dynamic speeches, and good ideas are well-read individuals who have developed their speaking ability. Public speaking is the most sought-after course in adult education today. This is a super-communication era of satellites, television, and personal assertiveness, yet the initial fear of public speaking is common to all of us.

Don't dodge the specter of public speaking any longer! Do the thing you fear and it will be the death of fear itself! Become a confident, vital speaker and conversationalist. It will put magic into your personality.

See the fun side. Another aid to a well-rounded personality is a good sense of humor. Buy some joke books or comedy albums. Listen to the comedians on television. Read the comic strips. Take a few humor books home from the library, or, better yet, buy some. Read them and study the art.

Learn some one-liners and a few short quips and anecdotes, and try them on friends. (Be sure to keep it short.) Work them into your conversations. Soon others will see a new side to you, the fun side.

Learn to listen. Another key to becoming a more sparkling personality is to be a better listener. Develop a pair of cauliflower ears. Listening is essential to leadership and a strong personality because it's only by emphatic listening that we can get to know others, their problems, needs, interests, and objectives. *If you're talking, you're not learning.*

Bernard Baruch, a statesman and a titan in the business world, offered this advice: "You can win more friends in two months by showing interest in others than you can in two years by trying to interest others in yourself."

How do you develop the art of listening? It takes deliberate work. Make a habit of looking at the people you're talking with. It's a quick turn-off to others when you don't look directly at them. Don't stare, but look at *them*, not the floor or the ceiling.

Force yourself not to interrupt or change the subject. It's fine to ask a question to clarify what the speaker is saying, but to interrupt before the other person is finished is just as rude as stepping on toes.

Learn to ask questions. Open-ended questions that can't be answered in just a few words are most useful. When you ask someone, "What do you do for hobbies and interests?" it will take them a while to answer you. You'll learn a lot. (And you'll also be complimented for your excellent personality!) Asking skillful questions and actively listening to the answers is conversational magic.

Develop your memory. Next, consider the miracle you carry around with you wherever you go. I call it your personal computer. I'm talking about your brain, the marvelous machine that makes the magic in your personality possible. The brain contains 11 billion nerve cells, each with some 25,000 inter-connections. Everything we've ever learned is stored there. Memory is a diary of life that we all carry with us. Man has created great wonders, but nothing that equals the human brain!

With a bit of work, you can improve your memory 300 to 400 percent and develop your retention of names, lists, facts, numbers, and ideas. Improving your memory will increase your self-confidence and peace of mind. All it takes is a system and continual practice.

Desire and concentration are essential to remembering. When you meet someone new, pay attention to the person's name. Spell it, repeat it, and write it down as soon as you have a chance. Review it until you know it. Try to make a mental association that will help you to remember it the next time you see that person.

My name can be associated with Robert Montgomery, the movie and TV star; or Montgomery Ward, the department store; or the famous WWII British field marshall, Bernard Montgomery. It helps to make these associations absurd, ridiculous, or exaggerated.

If you meet someone with the name of a friend, picture that new acquaintance shaking hands with your friend and it will help you to recall the name when you meet again.

Sometimes you can make up a rhyme to remind you of a name. If you meet someone named Jim Quinn, you could use the rhyme "Jim Quinn has a double chin" (if he were overweight) or "Jim Quinn drinks double gins" (if he were a drinker) or "Jim Quinn has to win" (if he were an obviously success-motivated person). Make a game out of it and practice recalling names through association wherever you go. Soon you'll be storing names away almost effortlessly and with great accuracy.

Maintain vitality. I've found that the most essential quality of a winning personality is vitality. The dictionary defines vitality as the characteristic that distinguishes the living from the non-living.

Whether you call it life, energy or enthusiasm, vitality is a magic ingredient for winning friends, having fun and achieving success. (Enthusiasm is infectious, so let's start an epidemic!)

How do you develop vitality and maintain it day in

and day out? A positive attitude is essential. Learn to give yourself pep talks any time, anywhere, day or night.

A pep talk is instant confidence. An effective pep talk is short, spirited, specific, and all-positive. It's a motivational faith talk with yourself. It can be as short and simple as "I'm a pro!" or "Ain't I great!" or "Get excited, Bob! Get going! Do your best!"

Speak vitally and emphatically to yourself, even though you may be talking silently. Make a regular habit of giving yourself pep talks. It will work magical wonders in your life. (My mother found it valuable to say to herself throughout the day, "Get the work; don't let the work get you!")

Watch your appearance. It is also important to pay attention to your appearance. Appearance is a real factor in communicating your personality to others. Whether you are selling, applying for a job, or meeting people for the first time in a non-business environment, you are being judged by first impressions. Your clothes, facial expression and posture all communicate something about you for good or ill.

Facial expression is an often neglected area. Many happy people forget to notify their faces. Shakespeare described this well when he wrote "The tartness of his face sours ripe grapes."

So remember to show a pleasant smile. A smile reflects confidence as well as a positive personality. Heed the Oriental saying: "She who cannot smile ought not to own a shop." Show your friendly side to others, and you will find that the people you meet will mirror your smile.

Accentuate the positive. As Appius Claudius said ages ago, "Every individual is the architect of his own fortune." Each of us has been gifted with talents. It is necessary only to develop a great confidence in yourself and in your own strengths and skills. Know that no one will ever value you more highly than you value yourself.

Benjamin Franklin worked methodically at rooting out the negative aspects of his character. Each year he wrote down what he considered to be 13 weaknesses in his personality. Then he worked on them one at a time for four weeks each. Since there are 13 four-week cycles in each year, each one of his lists occupied him for a whole year.

He worked on curbing his temper for four weeks; then on hearing others out before speaking; then on saying kind things; then on patience; then on being friendly.

How about making your own list and adopting this system to eliminate the bad traits and poor habits in your life?

You should also keep a current list of your talents, skills, and accomplishments. Discover what your ability is and maximize it. Look at your list frequently and affirm your positive traits. Follow the advice of the person who wrote the poem, "Believe in Yourself":

BELIEVE in yourself! Believe you were made
To do any task without calling for aid.
Believe, without growing too scornfully proud,
That you, as the greatest and least, are endowed.
A mind to do thinking, two hands and two eyes
Are all the equipment God gives to the wise.

BELIEVE in yourself! You're divinely designed
And perfectly made for the work of mankind.
This truth you must cling to through danger and
 pain:
The heights man has reached you can also attain.
Believe to the very last hour, for it's true,
That whatever you will you've been gifted to do.

BELIEVE in yourself and step out unafraid.
By misgivings and doubt be not easily swayed.
You've the right to succeed; the precision of skill
Which betokens the great you can earn if you will!
The wisdom of ages is yours if you'll read,
But you've got to believe in yourself to succeed.
                              —Author Unknown

William James, the 19th century psychologist, advised: "Let no individual have any anxiety about the upshot of his or her education, whatever the extent of it might be. If you keep faithfully busy day after day you'll wake up to be one of the competent ones of your generation."

When you are developing confidence and magic in your personality, it's important to keep aware of what's going on in the world. Keep up on business, government, religion, and sports. It's almost impossible to be a personable conversationalist without a keen awareness of current events.

Keeping abreast of what's going on means reading at least one daily paper and at least one weekly news magazine. It is wise to keep an ear on the radio and an eye on the television in the morning before heading for work and again on arriving home in the evening. TV is especially helpful. (As the Oriental saying reminds us, "One time seeing is worth a thousand times hearing.")

Try to master several subjects while keeping up on all the latest news. It is fine to have a thorough knowledge of one subject but you need a wide range of knowledge to be a good conversationalist.

•

If you were to ask me what is the most important quality for success in business, or for a winning personality, I would tell you *vitality*—vitality of voice, body and spirit. The second most important quality is *persistence.* Keep working at what you want. Keep planning for it and studying for it.

Always keep in your mind and heart the nine words Winston Churchill spoke to the youngsters at Harrow School in England when he returned to his alma mater in later years. He stirringly told the students: "Never give up! Never! Never! Never! Never! Never! Never!"

You'll be a V.P. if you practice vitality and persistence, two key principles for success. You'll be a V.I.P. if you add *initiative.* Initiative is the spirit needed to originate action. It is the characteristic of a decisive, active, positive personality.

Keep in mind the IDA formula to be more decisive. *I* is for an *idea* you have; *D* is for *decide* what you can and will do about it; *A* is for the necessary *action.*

An idea is of no more actual value than a kernel in a shell. Both are worthless unless you get them out and put them to use.

If you aren't enjoying life, it's no one's fault but your own. Your thoughts determine your success. Put some magic into your personality. Seek out friends. They're probably waiting to hear from you. Call them on the phone or visit them in person. Don't wait for others to call or drop by or write. Take the first step. You'll find that fun and happiness begin with giving of yourself, your ideas, your spirit, your talents.

Years ago the famous writer and editor Elbert Hubbard wrote: "Whenever you go out of doors, draw the chin in, carry the crown of the head high, and fill the lungs to the utmost. Drink in the sunshine. Greet your friends with a smile. And put soul into every handclasp. Keep your mind on the great and splendid things you'd like to do, and picture in your mind the able, earnest, useful person you'd like to be. Preserve a right mental attitude—the attitude of courage, frankness and good cheer." Hubbard crammed into one concise paragraph half a dozen ways to put magic into your personality now.

Harry Emerson Fosdick made a startling observation and wrote about it in a memorable analogy. He wrote that the Sea of Galilee and the Dead Sea are made of the same water. The Sea of Galilee makes beauty of its water. People swim, boat and fish there. Birds and plant life abound. The Sea of Galilee has an outlet. It gets to give. This sea gathers its riches that it may pour them out again to fertilize the Jordan plain.

But the Dead Sea has no outlet. It keeps all it has. It gives off a stench. There is no life there.

Psychologists tell us that people with many outlets, people with many friends, interests and hobbies, are happier, better balanced, more vibrant individuals. So get outside of yourself. Reach out to others. William James said: "The meaning of life is to spend it for something more important than self."

In the fifteenth century, Pico Della Mirancola wrote this paragraph which he titled "The Dignity of Man":

The great artisan created man with an undetermined nature, and then told him: you shall determine for yourself your own nature, in accordance with your own free will. Neither heavenly nor earthly in nature, you may fashion yourself in whatever form you shall prefer. You shall have the power to degenerate into the lower forms of life, which are brutish. But you shall also have the power, out of your own soul's judgment, to be reborn into higher forms, which are divine.

Good luck in putting magic into your personality. Work at it daily because a winning personality is an acquirement, not a gift.

ROBERT X. LEEDS

Robert X. Leeds is one of those fortunate individuals who has led a "charmed" existence.

Too young to enlist in the Army when World War II broke out, Leeds joined the Merchant Marine. Then, when he turned 17, he talked his way into the Army Cadet Training Program.

After his discharge he worked his way around the world, traveling extensively throughout Africa, Southeast Asia and China. While employed by the Israeli underground, Robert studied airborne tactics in Czechoslovakia and later trained and commanded the first Israeli Airborne Brigade during the 1947-1948 Middle East War. Both he and his Finnish wife were awarded medals for their service as foreign volunteers.

In 1949, Robert returned to the United States to complete the requirements for a bachelor's degree in industrial engineering and a master's degree in business administration.

After spending 17 years with America's largest automobile manufacturer, he resigned his position as director of industrial engineering services to establish his own concept for improving commercial pet care, a business called American Pet Motels.

In addition to teaching business management courses at graduate and undergraduate levels, Leeds is frequently sought to lecture on entrepreneurship opportunities.

His hobbies include flying, writing, and playing the organ. His first book is being considered for an animated TV special. A second book, a biographical novel, is nearing completion.

You may contact him by writing to Robert X. Leeds, 106 Stonegate, Buffalo Grove, IL 60090 or by telephoning (312) 634-9444.

ASK
AND YOU MAY RECEIVE

by ROBERT X. LEEDS

I've gotten used to people telling me that I am the luckiest person they ever met. Without the benefit of financial substance, influential parents, unique talents, or exceptional intelligence, I've managed to travel all over the world, receive a free college education, associate with leading political figures and Hollywood stars, and own a unique and prosperous business. When I needed a million dollars to start my business I walked into the office of one of America's richest men, whom I had never met before, and walked out with a blank check and a credit limit of $685 million.

For years I have listened to others tell me how close they came to "making it." Everyone, at one time or another, is presented with that golden opportunity. Unfortunately, most of us do not have the financial means or one of the other vital requisites necessary to seize the opportunity. Yet there is one missing link, the means of capitalizing on that opportunity, that may be pathetically close at hand. It is so obviously simple that few people exploit it. I am talking about asking somebody for something you want. Ask and you may receive.

•

A year ago, one of the Fortune 500 companies sold off all of its dog food manufacturing plants, leaving only their beautiful research kennel. The facility was too large and special to be of practical use to most people, but I knew it would make an ideal pet motel, which was the business I was in.

Since our company was in the midst of a touch-and-go public stock offering and all of our funds were tied up, I assumed that we didn't have the cash to make any kind of deal. But when the advertisement appeared repeatedly in the *Wall Street Journal,* I decided to invest 20 cents in a phone call.

"Make us an offer," pleaded the voice at the other end of the line. I decided to be honest with the other party and explained our cash situation.

"Mr. Leeds," the voice came back strongly, "Would you give us $50,000 for the land, the buildings, and all the equipment and supplies?"

Like the average person, I knew there had to be something wrong. So instead of saying yes, I flew to Iowa to inspect the property. It was more than I had even dreamed of. There was 6,000 square feet of ceramic tile buildings, a late model station wagon, and a tractor complete with all the apparatus to maintain the enclosed five-acre site. Inside the modern buildings were offices complete with a desk-top computer, modern steel desks, files, and electric typewriters. There was a complete laboratory with Bausch & Lomb microscopes and other scientific instruments. It was a total turn-key operation that I conservatively appraised at being worth half a million dollars. I accepted the deal at $50,000. I offered to give them $35,000 on Monday and the remaining $15,000 on the following Friday.

"No good," the seller replied. We must get the property off the books on Monday. If you can't raise more than $35,000 cash by Monday, we'll sell it to you for $35,000.

You can bet that I had $35,000 in an escrow account on Monday morning. Because I couldn't obtain the money from our corporate account, I borrowed the funds from a physician and agreed to pay him $5,000 for ten days' use of the money until my own funds were available. I never hesitate at the cost of doing business so long as the end result is favorable.

Was this spectacular opportunity a unique example? Not at all. I won't pretend to justify the financial logic of multi-national conglomerates. You don't have to understand the other party's situation in order to take advantage of an opportunity. One thing I do know is that you may ask and not receive. But if you do not ask, you *surely* won't receive!

•

I thought that my experience was due to mere luck until I was interviewed by a reporter from a major newspaper. For more than three hours he asked me the details of my various exploits. How did I meet Osa Johnson, the famous Africa explorer? How did I get to fly with Roscoe Turner, one of America's most famous aviation pioneers? How did I get into the Army Air Cadet Program when I was a high-school dropout? How did I meet Ray Kroc (founder of McDonald's hamburgers), let alone become his partner in American Pet Motels?

Finally the reporter looked up at me and said, "Mr. Leeds, do you see any single consistent factor in every one of your experiences that explains why you were successful?"

So many people had told me I was lucky that I was brainwashed into believing it. I replied, "Sure. I am a very lucky person!"

The reporter smiled and shook his head. "You didn't succeed because you were lucky. You succeeded because you were either *too naive* or *too simplistic* to accept that anything was impossible!"

The reporter drew his chair up close and spread his voluminous notes across the expanse of my desk. Beginning with my first experience, this stranger began to unravel a philosophy of enterprise which I now accept as one of the greatest reservoirs for potential anyone can imagine. Without realizing it, I had achieved amazing results by doing the simplest and most obvious thing in the world. It was so simple and obvious that everyone tended to overlook it: *When I needed or wanted something I couldn't afford, I wrote a letter asking if I could have the item on my terms.*

Does this approach work in any situation? Let me tell you it does! During the closing years of World War II, I desperately wanted to become a fighter pilot. The problem was that to be accepted in the Air Cadet Program you had to be 17 years old and a high-school graduate with a B+ grade-point average. I had just turned 17 but I was an 11th-grade high-school dropout with a D+ average. There was no way on earth I could qualify for any special program, let alone the Air Cadets.

Not knowing that it couldn't be done, I sat down and wrote a brief but sincere letter to the Commanding Gen-

230

eral of the United States Army Air Forces in Washington, D.C. I admitted that I had probably been one of the biggest goof-offs to ever grace the halls of Cass Tech, "but," I went on, "I love my country and more than anything in the world I want to serve it in its time of trial."

I told the general that if he would accept me into the Air Cadet training program, I would apply myself as I never had before and not let him down. Naive? Ridiculous? Maybe. But what was the harm in asking?

Two weeks later I received orders to attend the special testing center in Detroit, and on July 15, 1944, I was sworn in as the first and only non-high-school graduate in the Air Cadet Specialized Training Program. This same program provided me with a complete college education at government expense.

You may think that this was a singular experience, but I can assure you it wasn't. No matter how rigid the rules or how overwhelming the bureaucracy, *someone, somewhere, has the power to make an exception.* I never cease to be amazed at how often people tell me about the wonderful opportunities that they "had" to let go by because they didn't have the means to take advantage of the published terms. Did they contact the party and ask for suitable terms? No!

•

A more recent example occurred with my son, who learned at least one thing from me. Having been ordered back to Texas from his Air Force base in Korea, Marc decided that he would like to spend the remaining 13 months of his enlistment with his best buddy on the island of Guam. His Commander told him in no uncertain terms that it was impossible to revise orders with less than 30 days remaining. Recalling my letter-writing experience with the Air Force, Marc wrote a personal letter to the Commanding General of the Strategic Air Command. Two weeks later he received a personal reply from the General: "Dear Marc, I don't know why anyone would want to be stationed on Guam, but if you are willing to extend your enlistment by five months, I'll put you on Guam."

A short time later, to the amazement of his commanding officer and the other office personnel, Marc received special orders transferring him to Guam.

Who knows? Maybe you will be doing the other party a great service by offering to do something or to buy something even though your terms are far different from those originally stated. And, if you are going to ask, *ask the person at the top.* That's the person who can make the decisions and alter the terms!

•

As a child, I read the adventure stories of Osa and Martin Johnson, the famous Africa explorers. When I was discharged from the Air Force I went to New York and asked Ms. Johnson to let me work for her in Africa. It was one of numerous requests I have made that have been declined.

At that time, I wanted to go to Africa more than anything else, but without money or a guaranteed job, the only possibility of my getting a visa was to present a letter from a relative in Africa guaranteeing my welfare while in that country. Not having any relatives of my own in Africa, I wrote to the uncle of a stranger I had met at the Y.M.C.A.

In two weeks I had two letters back. One was the letter which satisfied the visa requirements and the other was an invitation to be the guest of this family while visiting Africa. During the following two years I traveled the length and breadth of Africa, across Southeast Asia, and up into China. It was an odyssey few persons dare to dream about—all because I dared to write a letter and invest a few pennies in an airmail stamp.

•

Certainly this philosophy isn't always successful, but it has worked enough times for people I have met that I know it's bound to work for you. To be successful you have to accept that this world is full of opportunities and more than just a few nice people who are willing to help you succeed if you'll only give them the chance. But they are not going to seek you out. You are going to have to contact them!

This became more than evident while I was doing postgraduate study at Wayne State University. I was called upon to help line up a series of speakers for the School of Business Administration. When the lists were compared, mine read like *Who's Who in the World of Business*. "Ridiculous," was the consensus of the committee members.

"How do you know?" I answered. "Let me write them and see."

As a result of my correspondence, over the next two years we students were exposed to the business philosophy of vice presidents, presidents, and board chairmen of many of America's largest corporations, including General Motors, Avis, and Chrysler. In addition, our meetings grew into banquets which attracted a host of other business and civic leaders, including the governor. What did it cost to engage such a distinguished group of speakers? Not one penny. Winston Morrow, Semon Knudsen, and most of the other great, successful business leaders were at one time just like you and me. Sharing their knowledge to help others succeed is another dimension of their true greatness. But let the sycophant beware! Don't confuse this technique with begging for undeserved riches or unwarranted attention. A less-than-honest interest is doomed to failure.

•

Is there a particular type of person or company that can be approached in this way and another that cannot? I don't believe so. Even the most staid and conservative institution is vulnerable. I know of one instance where a young man with a $400 credit-card limit took a trip abroad and managed to run up a bill of several thousand dollars before his credit was shut off. At the same time he realized that he had over-extended himself to the point where he could not possibly make the required payments.

Fearing that he might lose his job and suffer other kinds of economic consequences, the youth considered every form of alternative. Finally, in abject despair, he wrote to the president of the issuing bank explaining his predicament and asking that he be permitted to undertake an unusually long-term payment plan. He was astute enough to enclose his mutilated credit card in the same envelope.

During the first few years his monthly remittance barely covered the interest charge. Several years later he finally made his last payment, and a month after that he received a new credit card in the mail. His new credit limit was $2000!

What did this young man stand to lose by asking for special terms that most of us would have considered absurd? Was default more conscionable? He had nothing to lose and everything to gain. He asked and he received! Today he is an officer of a small corporation and has signature authorization for the company's checks. Had he not written that letter the story might have had a much different ending.

•

A different kind of example involves Donald M. Dible, the editor and publisher of this series. When Don wrote his first book, the now famous *Up Your OWN Organization!*, he recognized the tremendous marketing challenge he was facing. He had no credentials as an author. He had never published anything before, and for that matter, he had never written anything for publication before. But he didn't want a good book to fail on that account. It didn't take a lot of foresight for him to appreciate that an introduction or foreword by some well-known person would enhance the book's marketability.

When *Up Your OWN Organization!* was published, it bore not only an introduction by Robert Townsend, former Chairman of the Board of Avis Rent-A-Car Corporation, but also a foreword by the internationally famous industrialist, William P. Lear, Board Chairman of Lear Motors Corporation.

How much did Dible pay these two well-known celebrities? Not a single penny. Don dared to write a request to each of these gentlemen. He asked one to write the introduction and the other to write the foreword, hoping for one of the men to respond favorably. He was pleasantly surprised when both men agreed. Obviously the association of these two well-known entrepreneurs with his book was not wholly responsible for making the book the bestseller it has become, but Don would be the first to agree that it certainly didn't hurt. He risked nothing by seeking the best. He asked and he received!

•

One of my greatest experiences involved the creation of my present business, the American Pet Motels. Although there are some very dedicated people in the pet-boarding industry, for a long time I had felt that most boarding operations were unprofessional, unethical, and in some respects totally unscrupulous. Driven by the desire to change this image, I resigned an executive position it had taken me 17 years to attain and devoted all my energy to designing a total pet-boarding concept. That meant giving up fat bonus checks, five new company cars a year, and all the security and pension that went along with being an executive with one of America's largest manufacturing corporations.

Two years later I had the marketing plans, the building blueprints, and everything else I needed to start my business except the million dollars necessary for the land and construction. I visited every bank and loan institution in Michigan and Illinois, only to learn that venture capital for a start-up business was then non-existent. For something as far out as a million-dollar motel for animals, it probably never did exist.

If I had had the common sense of the average person, I would have recognized the impossible and given up right then. Instead, I wrote a letter to a fellow I had never met. According to what I had read about him, he had been pretty successful in transforming a ten-cent hamburger into a billion-dollar restaurant chain called McDonald's.

One week later I walked out of Ray Kroc's office in Oakbrook, Illinois, with a million-dollar line of credit and a new business partner. Today American Pet Motels is a thriving and prosperous prototype for a chain of pet motels that are planned for every major metropolitan area in America.

What did I have to lose by asking a stranger for some advice? Was it presumptuous of me? Perhaps. But consider what I stood to lose by giving up. And what possible harm was there in seeking the expert advice of a man who had already proven his competence? Was I lucky?

Certainly. But luck did not enter into it until after I had posed the question to Ray Kroc and he had evaluated the merits of my idea.

You may be sitting on either the idea of the century or the greatest waste of time and effort your spouse ever tolerated. Which one it turns out to be will ultimately be decided by whether you continue to roost on it or take some positive step to bring it to reality.

•

What kind of people might you expect to find out there at the other end of your requests? You might expect the people who receive such letters to scoff at their contents, at best to merely discard them in the waste basket after reading. (I'm sure this has happened to some of my letters, if they were read at all.) But, obviously, this is not always the case. Let me give you one last example of the kind of person you may encounter.

Quite recently I wrote a short Christmas story about Santa Claus and his dog, and it ended up being published in book form. I had never intended to write the story, much less have it published. A friend to whom I had given a copy passed it on to a lady who was grieving over the recent loss of her own dog. This lady, in turn, showed the book to her son, who worked for Walt Disney Studios. At a cocktail party the son suggested the book to an animator who was looking for a story for a TV Christmas special.

So it happened that I received an enthusiastic call from this producer, offering to produce the film on a joint-venture basis—providing that I pay the cost of providing a good narrative sound track. The man even suggested the names of a few local radio commentators whom I had never heard of. Now it seemed to me that if an unknown author and an unknown producer were

237

going to try to market an untested film, they ought to have someone really famous to do the narration.

For me there was only one choice—the man that I believe is one of the greatest talents living, Orson Welles. I obtained his agent's telephone number from the public library and immediately telephoned him.

My spirits were crushed when I learned that Orson Welles can command as much as $100,000 just to read a script before deciding if he will do it. Moreover, while Welles had consented to do a number of TV commercials, he had declined any serious film work for the past several years, preferring to write and direct. His minimum fee was $15,000 a day, and there was no guarantee that he could complete a one-hour reading in one day or even one week!

I was almost distraught, and at the other end of the line Arnold Weissberger must have sensed my disappointment.

"Mr. Leeds," I heard his voice calling, "Mr. Leeds, Orson Welles is a very rare and fine gentlemen. Let me make a suggestion. I'll give you Orson's home address. If you really feel your story is good, send him a copy of your book and tell him what you can afford to offer him. Then, let him make the decision."

I had been so consumed by the seeming hopelessness of the situation that I had almost decided to give it up. Then, suddenly, I realized that I was falling into that old trap. I was giving up without even trying. What did I have to lose by following my own cardinal rule—ask!

Once again I wrote a straightforward and honest letter to a total stranger. It took almost four weeks before I received in the mail a large package from Orson Welles. Was it my book being returned, or could it possibly be the sound track I so much desired? Opening the package, I was ecstatic to find the completed sound track for the entire film! Welles' rendering of the narration defies description. No one could have equaled his performance!

The total cost? Orson Welles, probably the greatest narrative voice of our time, charged me $90, the actual tape cost. In accord with my offer, I will send him the balance of the money when the film is completed and sold.

•

I may be the eternal optimist, but I believe we exist in the midst of limitless opportunity. The greatest invention, the most valuable concept, the noblest idea—all are without value unless they are brought into being.

The poet claims that the pen is mightier than the sword; the pen also happens to be as good as any pick or shovel for mining gold! What do you have to lose by asking?

INTRODUCING
THE EDITOR:
DONALD M. DIBLE

Don Dible presents more than 100 speeches, seminars and workshops a year all across the United States under the sponsorship of universities, trade associations, chambers of commerce, business magazines, professional societies, and private companies.

His lucid, enthusiastic, experience-backed presentations are designed to inspire and motivate seminar participants and convention audiences to put to immediate use the highly-practical information he covers.

In preparing his talks, Don draws from a rich and varied background. He received his BSEE from MIT and his MSEE from Stanford University. Prior to launching his first business in 1971, he served in engineering and sales management capacities with three companies, including a subsidiary of the SCM Corporation, where he was responsible for directing and training a large national sales organization producing millions of dollars in sales annually.

In the past seven years, Don has founded eight successful businesses in the publishing, advertising, seminar, graphic arts services, and real estate industries. All but one of these companies was started on a part-time basis with modest capital resources. Each of Mr. Dible's businesses reflect the unusual and innovative approach he takes to sales, marketing and finance—topics discussed in detail during his many seminars and talks.

While Don is still blazing new trails in his speaking career, he is perhaps best known for his work in the field of publishing.

Prior to writing his 100,000-copy bestseller, *Up Your OWN Organization!*, Don had never written a single word for publication in his life. Aside from writing themes, book reports, and term papers in high school and college, his only major writing project was a highly technical undergraduate thesis at the Massachusetts Institute of Technology.

After working for seven years in industry, Don became frustrated with the rigidly structured world of big business. He looked longingly and lovingly at the outside world of entrepreneurship—and decided to launch his own business.

Following three years of research, including attendance at numerous seminars, interviews with hundreds of successful small business owner/managers, and a thorough review of the small business books in print at the time, (mostly dry-as-a-bone textbooks and rah-rah get-rich-quick books), he finally decided that the most needed new product in the marketplace was a *realistic* book about starting a new business. Faithful to his commitment, he raised the needed capital; and with the assistance of his dedicated wife he started The Entrepreneur Press. Next he hired a secretary, and in just four months produced a 750-page manuscript for *Up Your OWN Organization!*, with an Introduction by Robert Townsend, former Chairman of the

Board of Avis Rent-a-Car and bestselling author of *Up The Organization.* Don's second book is titled *The Pure Joy of Making More Money.*

Shortly after the publication of his first book, Don was asked to assist a professional society in organizing and presenting a two-day conference utilizing the services of fourteen attorneys, accountants, business consultants and financial executives. The program was recorded, the recordings were transcribed, and he edited and adapted the transcripts into manuscript form. The resulting book was titled *Winning the Money Game—How to Plan and Finance a Growing Business.*

As a result of the success of The Entrepreneur Press, Don has published (or is in the process of publishing) the following books: *Up Your OWN Organization!; Winning the Money Game; Everybody's Tooth Book; The Pure Joy of Making More Money; How to Make Money in Your Own Small Business; Fundamentals of Record-keeping and Finance for the Small Business; What Everybody Should Know about Patents, Trademarks and Copyrights; Business Startup Basics;* and *The Official U.S. Export-Import Guide.*

Recently Don founded a new publishing enterprise, the Showcase Publishing Company, dedicated to multi-author motivational and inspirational self-help books. This is the third volume published by this company.

Finally, Don has been a guest on scores of television and radio talk shows, including NBC's "Monitor," with Bill Cullen, and ABC's award-winning "Mike Wallace at Large." He is also a frequent contributor to magazines such as *Dun's Review, Success Unlimited, MBA Magazine, Free Enterprise,* and *Boardroom Reports.*

You may contact Don by writing to him at 3422 Astoria Circle, Fairfield, CA 94533, or by telephoning (707) 422-6822.

This book was designed & produced
by George Mattingly, at GM Design, Berkeley
from Trump Mediaeval & Friz Quadrata types
set by Robert Sibley, Abracadabra, San Francisco
and was printed & bound by R. R. Donnelley & Sons
Crawfordsville, Indiana.